THE

REAL
JESUS

BERT M. FARIAS

A Holy Fire Ministry Publication.
Printed in the United States of America.
ISBN-13: 978-0692876411
ISBN-10: 0692876413

Library of Congress data is available for this title.

CONTENTS

PREFACE

The real identity of the Church is in proportion to her identity with the real Jesus. But, too often, the believer's identity is with things pertaining to a form of Christianity based on doctrinal fads and theological biases or a leader's personality — shaped within a "Christian" subculture built on its own ideals, philosophies, and traditions, combined with a particular brand or flavor of God created in our own image, and not with Christ Himself.

"You thought I was altogether as thyself" — The Psalms

"It seems to me that, if we get one look at Christ in His love and beauty, this world and its pleasures will look very small to us." ~D.L. Moody~

"Much of our difficulty as seeking Christians stems from our unwillingness to take God as He is and adjust our lives accordingly. We insist upon trying to modify Him and to bring Him nearer to our own image." ~A.W. Tozer~

When we see Jesus as He is, glorious and worthy of our deepest loyalties and affections, deserving of our total focus and supreme attention; we will catch fire inwardly and burn with holy fear, and a holy hunger for the Word will grip our hearts, and we will proclaim Him as He is. ~Anonymous~

"There is a God we want, and there is a God who is... And they are not the same God." ~Patrick Morley~

"As a child, I received instruction both in the Bible and in the Talmud. I am a Jew, but I am enthralled by the luminous figure of the Nazarene. No one can read the gospels without feeling the actual presence of Jesus. His personality pulsates in every word. No myth is filled with such life." ~Albert Einstein~ *Saturday Evening Post*, Oct. 26, 1929

"The wicked have fashioned a god who will not hold them accountable." ~Carter Conlon~

"It is a painful process to discover that one has invested not in Jesus, but in one's theology about Jesus." ~Anonymous~

"Too many Christians want a manageable, domesticated Jesus who makes no demands on their time, money, words, social life, and sexuality. In the midst of this great and growing deception, God is looking for uncompromising believers who are committed to proclaiming the truth of the gospel and not the counterfeit Jesus of Western Culture." ~Anonymous~

"Too many of us have constructed a "god in a box," a god whose job is merely to pander to our needs, desires, and ambitions." ~Anonymous~

"We offer a motivational, pep-talk, feel-good, self-help, personal-empowerment Jesus rather than the Jesus of the Scriptures, and, in doing so, we damn our hearers rather than deliver them." ~Dr. Michael L. Brown~

Many are convinced they are faithful Bible believers but, in fact, worship a different Jesus — one contracted from a "revelation" they supposedly received from the latest "Christian" cultural fad or their favorite celebrity superstar preacher — an idolatrous, fantasy, and fictitious Jesus constructed subjectively in their own minds and built upon the sentiment of American values. Sooner or later we are going to have to come to grips with the Person and ethics of Jesus Christ and get serious about who He really is." ~Dr. Stephen Crosby~

"Sadly, I think many in the community of believers cling to an Americanized gospel which equates what is biblically true and reliable with being part and parcel of various right-wing political agendas. Actually, Christianity itself in the US and many other nations has been interpreted (and by virtue of this) rewritten to gel with sentiments and ideas that actually run contrary to what the Messiah taught and advocated (Torah-based Judaism), e.g., unbridled capitalism and the

greed it is predicated on and the corruption it engenders and promotes. I dare say if Yeshua HaMashiach physically visited most American churches, He would not recognize what was being taught and advocated as being remotely like what He articulated and lived."
~Dr. Anthony G. Payne~

In order to have the true image of Christ built into your spirit, you must consider the entire body of His life, example, and teachings. For instance, if you focus only on the account of Jesus going into the temple and overturning the tables of the moneychangers in a fit of righteous indignation and driving them out of the temple with a whip, you would be led to believe that Jesus is angry with people day and night. Your image of Him would be that He is looking for a reason to punish you instead of bless you. Having this mindset of the Son of God would make you think of Him as a religious fanatic filled with rage, which puts Him closer to being a candidate for anger-management classes. This image does not inspire love, faith, and praise in the human heart.

On the other hand, and this happens much more frequently, if you focused your image of Him on His encounter and exchange with the adulterous woman whom the scribes and the Pharisees wanted to stone, you probably would come to the conclusion that Jesus never gets angry, never judges, and is just the sweetest, most gentle person. This image would probably cause you to act presumptuously, believing that Jesus always understands you and your sinful issues and will let you get away with anything. This mindset would eventually lead you to believe and live in an unscriptural mercy. In the West and nations that have been influenced by the false western gospel, this is the image of Jesus most are familiar with, and their conduct is derived from such a one-sided perception.

Yet neither conclusion would be right within itself, because both sides are Him, and we can know Jesus and His Person only as we study the full body of His life and teachings.

If most Christians represented the real Jesus, many people would more easily believe in Him, for, when He is presented in the true light of the Scriptures, the average human heart would be irresistibly drawn to Him. But this is exactly the problem, as John Pavlovitz writes:

"For far too many people, being a Christian no longer means you need to be humble or forgiving. It no longer means you need a heart to serve or bring healing. It no longer requires compassion or mercy or benevolence. It no longer requires you to turn the other cheek, or to love your enemies, or to take the lowest place, or to love your neighbor as yourself. It no longer requires Jesus."

"When I quit identifying as a Christian a few years ago, it felt like I became a part of the human race. I had the ear of those who were turned off by the religion of Christianity and their genuine friendship as well. People would rather see Jesus than be told about Him (when they see Him they'll want to hear about Him). Most people don't reject the real Jesus; they reject the Jesus that is represented by people who don't really know Him and follow Him."

What we behold is what we eventually become.

When we behold the glory of the Lord as in a mirror (this means, at least in part, to behold Him in the mirror of His Word and by the Spirit's unveiling of Him to your spirit), we will be gradually transformed by the Holy Spirit into that same glory and reflect the brightness of that image out to the world.

"But we all, with unveiled face, beholding as in a mirror the glory of the Lord, are being transformed into the same image from glory to glory, just as by the Spirit of the Lord" (2 Cor. 3:18).

A PROPHECY CONCERNING THIS ASSIGNMENT

"It is time now to step deeper into the waters of the baptism of a mature son. The transformation in you shall be great. You will love with the love of Another, and your knowledge of the Son shall greatly increase. Your understanding of His heart to please the Father shall increase. You shall take much delight in the beauty of His holiness. His great love for complete obedience to the Father shall be revealed to you

and in you, and this love of obedience shall become your own.

The beauty of the meekness of the soul of the Son of man shall become your consuming desire. The words of the Father, "This is My beloved Son in whom I am well pleased," shall take on new meaning.

Yes, you shall write with deeper levels of anointing now as you remain in the secret place of the Son. Yes, you shall write about the beauty of the Son and His holiness, and as you do, I will make Him desirable to My people. And by revelation of this anointing, they shall come to know the meaning of Him who is called "the Desire of all nations."

Behold the pattern Son! Behold the Beloved One! Behold what you shall become! Go and study the life of My Son. Observe Him in the gospels. Observe Him in the life of Paul, who had understanding of the mystery of the Son. Let this quiet confidence which is beginning to be birthed in you come to blossom in the revelation of My Son. This is the anchor of your soul. This is the mind of Christ."

CHAPTER 1

HOW MUCH OF CHRIST IS IN YOUR CHRISTIANITY?

That's quite a compelling question, isn't it? It's kind of like asking how much of Christ is in Christmas. I think many of us would agree that Christmas has become so commercialized that Christ is hardly noticed, much less celebrated and revered. Easter would be in the same category. How in the world a celebration of the resurrection of Jesus Christ could've ever evolved into an affinity with Easter bunnies and Easter eggs, I'll never know. Such is the tenuous nature of idolatry.

Is it possible for Jesus Christ to be lost in Christianity, the very religion whose name it bears and professes? We know that, without a relationship with Christ, just another religion is all that remains. We also know from scripture that someone can profess to know Christ but in works actually deny Him (Tit. 1:16). But isn't it also true that, in works, many may profess to know Him, but in authentic heart knowledge they do not?

Who knew Jehovah in Old Testament times? That earthly system of Judaism was to point the way to Christ, but, in actuality, it hid Him from the multitudes, who were enmeshed in the works of the Law. The external had glossed over the need for the internal. Sin and death reigned in the old order of the Law and all its rituals, ceremonial rules, and customs.

Isn't the same true today? There is an external order in modern Christianity that seems to rule. Its emphasis on appearance, hype, professionalism, showmanship, and production easily allows us to deceive ourselves into thinking that, somehow, all these things become essential to our success — while Christ Himself is glossed over.

Many of our contemporary churches have become echo chambers for the latest trends in pop psychology, marketing, politics, entertainment, and entrepreneurial leadership, while the simple demands of Christ are often overlooked or packaged in a way to make Him palatable to the masses.

We have become all too enamored with our own glory in the kingdoms that we are building, at times totally unaware of receiving that invisible kingdom *"that cannot be shaken"* (Heb. 12:2).

Judaism, with all its external forms, rituals, and framework, began its forced removal 2,000 years ago and was replaced with a spiritual, heavenly standard established in the New Covenant. And now, in *this* end time, we are seeing once again the removal of all that is external to bring us forcibly to a certain point, and it is this:

After all is said and done, how much of the Christ do you really have? Not what you do, not what you've built, not what you have — not even the noble activities which constitute your Christian life. But how much of *the Christ Himself* have you got?

BEWARE

"Beware lest anyone cheat you through philosophy and empty deceit, according to the tradition of men, according to the basic principles of the world, and not according to Christ" (Col. 2:8).

Here in this chapter, Paul is speaking of the *inward* life, encouraging *the Christ life* — to walk in Him, and to be rooted and built up in Him. He is warning us of philosophies and empty deceits, based on traditions of men, and the basic principles of the world that speak to us of humanistic things, mystical things, and outward things that are without real, eternal substance. Much like today and throughout the centuries of time, Christianity can too easily slip into an outward-ness. *"Don't be cheated,"* Paul says, out of the simplicity and completeness of the inward Christ life. There are many things that seek to rob, steal, and plunder our love, affection, and holy, intimate knowledge of the Lord Jesus Christ.

It is not just the philosophies and empty deceits we need to beware of, but there are even good and acceptable things, which, while having their proper place in the Christian life, have a tendency to cheat us out of the real person and mind of Christ. Such things as buildings, budgets, programs, projects, meetings, committees, or other things that concern the church system apart from the mind of Christ, have the potential to *dry up* the real heart of the Christ life. Often it's these very things that rob us of the hallowing intimacy which we are to experience with Christ. These things, although useful, must be kept in their proper perspective, lest they dilute the vision of Jesus Himself.

When Christ was born, a hellish opposition immediately arose to attempt to kill and destroy Him. Likewise, when the corporate counterpart of the Christ, the Man-child Company, is brought forth near the end of this age (Rev. 12), there will be yet another most violent release of hellish opposition. *"Little children, it is the last hour; and as you have heard that the Antichrist is coming, even now many antichrists have come, by which we know it is the last hour"* (1 Jn. 2:18).

Everything of this world order is in direct opposition to the Christ being revealed in reality and power.

The return of the Lord will once again signal the removal of all that is earthly, temporal, and of man, so that only the eternal order of Jesus Christ and His kingdom remains.

When Christ returns, He is coming for the formation of Christ in us. It is Him in us that He will recognize. His words, *"I never knew you,"* and *"I don't know you"* were spoken to so-called ministers and foolish virgins who were doing the work of God and who laid claim to His name (Mt. 7:23) (Mt. 25:12). Somehow, the Christ was not found in them. Somehow, their form of Christianity had replaced Christ Himself.

So, once again, the question beckons us: How much of Christ is in your Christianity?

CHAPTER 2

IS THE CHURCH'S IDENTITY IN CHRIST ALONE?

The Holy Spirit will minister fresh revelation to your heart as you seek Jesus. After all, one of the Spirit's main functions is to glorify Jesus and testify of Him (Jn. 16:13-14; 15:26), and to lead you and guide you into all truth.

My wife and I have been in the ministry for three decades. We are still growing in our intimate knowledge of the Lord through His Word and an ever-increasing experience. There is an ache and a hunger inside of us for a newer and simpler expression of Christ in our lives. In many ways, as some of you have also done, from the time of our new birth, we've had to leave the many traditions, structures, and systems of men to discover and re-discover Jesus. Removing the layers of religion and tradition that gloss over the pure and clear image of Christ Himself is a lifelong process. For us, even the profession of ministry no longer has the appeal it had years ago, having been replaced by a purer desire to simply build His kingdom in a Christ-centered way in the context of God-ordained relationships, being rooted and established in Him alone.

Our heavenly Father is preparing His family and His army for that which is to come on the earth. *"But know this, that in the last days perilous times will come…"* (2 Tim. 3:1). *"But the end of all things is at hand; therefore be serious and watchful in your prayers."* (1 Pt. 4:7). In light of the coming gross darkness that is increasing on the earth, we believe the glory of the Lord will also increase that much more. In the days ahead, the true Church will look vastly different than it does right now. We are longing for His glory and the restoration of all things (Acts 3:21) and praying earnestly: *"Thy kingdom come, thy will be done on earth as it is in heaven."*

My wife and I feel like we've been going through a process of metamorphosis of late. You could say that our personal constitution is being radically altered. We're asking heart-searching questions that we were once afraid to ask. These questions may disturb some who have grown comfortable in their controlled habitats and predictable environs, but they beckon to be asked and answered.

This current phase of our journey began with one question and then many that subsequently followed. How did 3,000 new converts on the day of Pentecost move from their conversion to continuing steadfastly in their newfound faith — from Acts 2:41 to Acts 2:42? Without buildings, without budgets, without paid staff, and without a head pastor, how was the early Church able to function and disciple a harvest of 3,000 new people? Not 30; not even 300; but 3,000! Then, two chapters later, another 5,000 men were added to their company (Acts 4:4).

What if churches today lost their buildings? Could they still function as churches? If there was war, or a great crisis, or severe persecution against the Church, as there could very well be in the very near future of America, could they still function as a church? Would churches be able to continue meeting as spiritual families and bodies in fellowship, teaching, worshipping, praying, and taking care of one another without a large facility? Would the believers throughout a city or region stay connected? Are our connections based on a physical facility or simply on relationship with the Lord and with each other? Or would the loss of a building mean the essential loss of the church?

What if a large church today lost its budget, or paid staff, or senior pastor? Would there still be shepherds to care for the sheep? Or would there be hirelings looking for professional "ministry" elsewhere?

What if a church lost its denominational affiliation? Would it cease to exist? Or if a non-denominational church dropped their seeker-friendly philosophy or in-vogue style of "doing church," or their various programs that attract people, would they still exist as a church? How much of our dependence have we placed on these things? And perhaps the biggest question upon which hangs all other questions is this: Without any of these things, could the Church still have its identity in Jesus alone?

Here's a great challenge:

Turn off the electricity at your corporate gathering for 30 days except for necessary lights for safety. Turn off the electric band with all the instruments, the video displays, the fancy and attractive graphics and effects. I'm not saying these things are wrong and unnecessary. I'm saying we should try to do without them only as an experiment that could lead to great self-discovery and a forthcoming renewed focus and change. Although the deception is more than just "electrical," you will quickly find out where the gathering is really at in the Lord. What happens when the band is no longer performing the latest, greatest "worship" songs that attract many. What happens when all the artificial perks are gone? Don't be surprised if, over the 30-day period, people start finding the exits to the building far more attractive. But then again, they could also start finding the Lord alone far more attractive as they remove the outward effects and artificial enhancements that hinder our total dependence on the Lord and His Spirit. It is most notable that, in many third-world countries, God is moving powerfully without all the "artificial help."

It can be a painful process to discover that one has invested not in Jesus, but in one's theology about Jesus. This discovery, however, can lead to a revolutionary change that will produce the peaceable fruit of true righteousness in those who are trained by such an exercise.

The aforementioned questions are not easy questions, but here is the bottom line: How much of Christ do we have in our lives, our relationships, our churches, and our ministries? After all has been said and done, after we strip away all the props that are holding up these modern churches, how much of the Church's identity and character is found in Jesus Christ alone?

My point is not to be critical of any existing church or ministry. I have no axe to grind or bone to pick. There are many good churches doing wonderful things for the Lord, and we are grateful for that. We should never criticize another man's labors but instead rejoice wherever Christ is proclaimed.

On the other hand, churches should be living extensions of Christ Himself, but too often they are extensions of pop culture, denominational traditions, or the leader's personality. In these cases, they depend more on their own ability to keep the church going. In doing so, we are declaring that helpful things such as buildings and budgets and programs become more necessary and essential for functioning than the workings of the Spirit of God and His people.

I am not saying that all the amenities aforementioned here are not helpful and useful, but if a church cannot exist without them, then I would say that you have an inflexible wineskin that cannot contain the likely probability of an expanding national crisis and the anticipated outpouring of the Spirit's richly condensed wine.

Let's be honest. Many of our churches today have either become museums or monuments that celebrate the past, or Fortune 500-styled, consumer-based corporations that can too easily exert themselves without the power of the Holy Spirit. Peripheral factors have become so deeply engrained in our methodology that we cannot fathom "doing church" without them. We cannot even imagine Jesus doing His work without these amenities. It makes me wonder whether many of our churches today are really Christ-centered or more consumer driven. I'm afraid we've substituted catering to people's felt needs over catering to God's demands. Keeping people happy has become essential, but the demands of Jesus have become optional.

Personally, I believe we have begun to see a revolution of sorts in the Church. God is moving in an unprecedented way across the globe, but it is happening below the radar of the traditional church, in a very quiet manner. Out of a deep spiritual dissatisfaction and a great hunger for God, true followers of Jesus are leaving traditional church systems at an alarming rate across denominational and non-denominational lines. Many are not happy with their spiritual lives. The problem is not really their church — it's just "church" in general.

Even though we've been in ministry for many years, we've sensed the same thing. There is a larger process of work God is doing in His people. He is bringing focus to Jesus and His kingdom. From all walks of life and church spectrums, people are searching for something more, but most of them don't quite know what that is.

Recently, in prayer, the Lord showed my wife and me two church worlds — a surface and an underground one. The surface church had many limitations governed by the systems and structures of men, but the underground church was full of people hungry for the presence of God, relationship with one another, and training and discipleship in the Word and ways of the Spirit.

In addition to some direction and instructions the Lord gave us, He also issued a strong warning not to be critical of other men's labors, especially those within the traditional system, but to judge the fruit only.

Be much in prayer, beloved, for everything that can be shaken will be shaken in this hour. May the Lord grant us much grace and wisdom for the times.

CHAPTER 3

AN IMAGINARY CHRIST

Before me now, I see the impression I saw years ago. There are two scenes. One is of a clear and sunny horizon, lined with an endless multitude of people. The other is of a vast forest, with no one in sight. Dense fog covers the forest, and out of the fog comes the Lord Jesus Christ. Christ, for the most part, is not found among the general populace. People have to really look to discern Him.

Think about it. Our Savior was not born in a big metropolis, but in the small town of Bethlehem. And He grew up in the despised country of Galilee. He was not born in a palace where kings lived, but in a lowly stable. The wise men had to really search and diligently follow the star to find Him. When Jesus entered into public ministry, it is written that He had no place to lay His head (Lk. 9:58). He did not have a ministry headquarters. He died a criminal's death on a cross, naked and nearly alone. His grave was a borrowed tomb. His throne was an invisible one, hidden from the multitudes of those who were taught, touched, healed, and delivered through His ministry. He was called "meek" and "lowly" — certainly not a description fitting for a king.

If you, like so many others, were looking for Him in the external, you'd miss Him. If you were looking for Him to come a certain way, in a certain form, according to a certain brand of theology, or doctrine, or a denominational view, packaged according to a set of certain traditional ideals, you'd miss Him again. *"Where have you hid my Lord?"* We've subtly hidden Him behind our forms, our façades, and our fads. We've masked Him from the multitudes who need to know Him as He is.

And why have we hid Him? Is it not for the same reason that He had no place to lay His head? Because He makes us too uncomfortable the way He is. He deals with our hearts, our attitudes, and our manner of life. He speaks the truth in love. He searches our motives and looks deep within. We don't like that. It's too uncomfortable.

We don't want our controlled habitats and boundaries we've created upset by Him. We don't want His glory to disturb our traditions and way of doing things. We allow Him to visit us occasionally, but He can't stay. If He did, we'd have to change the rules and play by His instead.

So what do we do? We design our own sanctuary or create our own culture and put Him there. We corral Him and control Him and place Him within our own boundaries and by-laws. We make Him one of us. We make Him fit into our lifestyle, our doctrine, our denomination, our traditions, and our culture. We make Him cool and hip. We make Him like us.

"To the female novelist, He is the romantic Christ. To the half-converted cowboy, He is the sentimental Christ, or worse yet, the Man Upstairs. To the academic egghead, He is the philosophical Christ. To the effeminate poet, He is the cozy Christ. To the all-star athlete, He is the muscular Christ. To the celebrity artist or popular actor, He is the cool and hip Christ." (partial quote from A.W. Tozer)

How radically different those images are from the way the apostle John saw Jesus in a vision near the end of his life:

"Then I turned to see the voice that spoke with me. And having turned I saw seven golden lampstands, and in the midst of the seven lampstands One like the Son of Man, clothed with a garment down to the feet and girded about the chest with a golden band. His head and hair were white like wool, as white as snow, and His eyes like a flame of fire; His feet were like fine brass, as if refined in a furnace, and His voice as the sound of many waters; He had in His right hand seven stars, out of His mouth went a sharp two-edged sword, and His countenance was like the sun shining in its strength. And when I saw Him, I fell at His feet as dead. But He laid His right hand on me, saying to me, "Do not be afraid; I am the First and the Last. I am He

who lives, and was dead, and behold, I am alive forevermore. Amen. And I have the keys of Hades and of Death." (Rev. 1:12-18).

John saw Jesus in all His majestic strength and splendor. So mighty and overwhelming was the glory of His presence that John could no longer stand on his feet. Today, most people have no idea of the fullness of Christ's glorious identity. To many, He is just a picture on the wall, a cross around their neck, or a stone statue in front of a church building, essentially having no real relevance or significance in their everyday lives. As Aaron did with the golden calf, they mold and fashion a god according to their own image and liking. They craft a god to meet their needs, and then they stick a "Jesus" label on their man-made idol. May God help us idolatrous earthlings see the real Jesus.

Here are some popular man-made Western versions of Jesus today:

1. **The Rolex Jesus.** Many people worship at the altar of this golden calf. This Jesus promises health, wealth, mansions and luxury cars — but the people who benefit most from his favors are the prosperity preachers who demand that you tithe to them.

2. **The Santa Claus Jesus.** He lives far, far away and visits rarely. He makes a list and checks it twice, and his love is based on your performance. If you aren't too naughty, he gives you what you ask for.

3. **The Rabbit Foot Jesus.** Some people treat Jesus like a magic charm. They don't seek to know him personally, but they figure if they show up at a church service a few times a year or hang a picture of him on their wall, they'll be lucky when bad things happen to other people.

4. **The Oprah Jesus.** He's soft, cuddly, and adaptable to your spiritual preferences. He lets you define your own morality. He's like a spiritual bartender — he'll mix Buddhism, Hinduism, and hedonism into your favorite New Age cocktail. He invites you to eat, drink, and be merry, because *all* religions lead to heaven.

5. **The Fightin' Fundie Jesus.** He's always angry, especially at

homosexuals, women who work outside the home, and stores that sell liquor on Sundays. At any moment, he's ready to unleash an earthquake to destroy America. He doesn't really like other countries, either.

6. **The Liberal Mainline Jesus**. He's similar to the Oprah Jesus, but more respectable. He doesn't mind if you rewrite the Bible, but he requires that you wear a suit to church and that you sing the first, second, and fourth verse of every hymn. And he asks that you keep your music very mellow.

7. **The Rock Star Jesus**. This one is hugely popular today. He doesn't care how you live your life during the week or who you sleep with, but, in church, you must be trendy and use lots of hair gel. Songs must be loud (even if they have no content), and sermons must have a lot of movie clips. Words such as "sin" or "holiness" are off-limits because they are just not cool.

8. **The Republican Jesus**. When this flag-waving Jesus was transfigured, he appeared with George Washington and Ronald Reagan. He's willing to bend the rules and let certain conservative politicians and pundits into heaven (especially Mormons) if they promise to keep taxes low and guns available.

9. **The Democratic Jesus**. He rides on a donkey and dispenses good will, health care, and stimulus money to all who are weary and heavy-laden. He steals from the rich, gives to the poor, and creates jobs for people who are too lazy to work. He's fine if you talk about God in speeches, as long as you don't mention sin or offend a special-interest group. *(Borrowed with permission from an article written by Lee Grady, one-time editor of Charisma magazine)*

I'm sure there are many other false versions of Jesus in our society and the world, but these are sufficient to make my point. There is such a great need today for the unveiling of the intimate, holy knowledge of the *real* Jesus.

Oh, people — do you see what we've done with the Holy One?

We've brought Him down to our level and made Him so common. Yes, he was made a common man, but yet so uncommon. No man ever lived like Him. No man ever loved like Him. No man ever spoke like Him. He was full of grace and truth (Jn. 1:14). He spoke from the fullness of the Godhead. All His words were the purest of wisdom. His works were the purest of power. His motives were the purest of love. He was the perfect man — not like us, but sent to make us like Him. Instead we've tried so hard to make Him like us.

Listen again to more of A.W. Tozer's revealing words:

"We serve a God today who very rarely ever astonishes anybody. He manages to stay pretty much within the constitution. Never does He break our bylaws. He's a very well-behaved God and very denominational and very much one of us, and we ask Him to help us when we're in trouble and watch over us when we're asleep. The God of the pretentious believer isn't a God I could have much respect for. But when the Holy Ghost shows us God as He is, we admire Him to the point of wonder and delight."

When was the last time you were filled with wonder and delight at the sight of Him? Have you been filled with the Spirit to even be able to see Him that way?

There are a great many "bogus Christs" among us these days. John Owen, the old Puritan, warned people in his day: *"You have an imaginary Christ, and if you are satisfied with an imaginary Christ, you must be satisfied with an imaginary salvation."*

Are you serving an imaginary Christ?

Here is another comparison that may help you to answer that question.

COMPARING THE BIBLICAL JESUS WITH THE POSTMODERN JESUS

1. The Biblical Jesus was born as God Almighty in the flesh, but the postmodern Jesus was born as a man promoted to Deity.

2. The Biblical Jesus warns us of sin, judgment, and hell, but the postmodern Jesus never says anything negative.

3. The Biblical Jesus commands repentance from sin, but the postmodern Jesus disregards the message of repentance.

4. The Biblical Jesus gives you salvation, hope, peace, and joy, but the postmodern Jesus gives you happiness, wealth, and sentimental feelings.

5. The Biblical Jesus was hated and despised by the world, but the postmodern Jesus is loved and accepted by the world.

6. The Biblical Jesus hates sin and exposes the truth about sin, but the postmodern Jesus condones sin and never confronts it.

7. The Biblical Jesus commands with Divine authority, but the postmodern Jesus offers "suggestions" instead of *Commandments*.

8. The Biblical Jesus offends the world with truth, but the postmodern Jesus hates to offend you and loves political correctness.

9. The Biblical Jesus brings division when necessary, but the postmodern Jesus promotes unity and tolerance at all costs.

10. The Biblical Jesus preaches God's righteousness, but the postmodern Jesus preaches only on sentimental love.

11. The Biblical Jesus exalts God the Father's will, but the postmodern Jesus serves your will, not God's will.

12. The Biblical Jesus warns of false signs and wonders and magnifies God's Word, but the postmodern Jesus exalts false signs, wonders, and mysticism above God's Word.

13. The Biblical Jesus demands that emotion, experience, and opinion conform to His Word and sound doctrine, but the postmodern Jesus exalts emotion, experience, and opinion above His Word and sound doctrine.

14. The Biblical Jesus commands you to deny yourself and allow

Christ to work in you, but the postmodern Jesus encourages you to love yourself and gratify all your fleshly desires.

Once again, the question beckons to be asked: Are you serving an imaginary Jesus or the real One?

CHAPTER 4

THE LOVE OF APPEARANCE

A moral and spiritual crisis marks 21st-century Western Christianity. It is ironic how, with so much knowledge at our fingertips, Biblical illiteracy seems to be at an all-time high. We have multi-translation Bibles, millions of Christian books, video and audio resources, and digital materials available on the Internet. We have celebrity television preachers, along with tens of thousands of churches that dot our landscape. Yet with all these resources so readily available to us, people are still easily duped and deceived by the hype and the hoopla, the glitter and the gold, the superficiality and the showmanship that marks so much of Western Christianity today, not to mention the many wolves in sheep's clothing that stalk our land.

The visible church in the mainstream of this once-great United States of America is gradually becoming a hollow echo even with its million-dollar edifices, high-tech media, and silver-tongued orators. People are putting their faith in the wisdom of men and in their charisma, eloquence, persuasive words, clever phrases, and logical dissertations. The demonstration of the Spirit and power of God operating through humble, broken men is fading. But God has reserved far better for those who possess an intimate knowledge of Him. They will do exploits (Dan. 11:32).

As a compelling example of the hollow-echo effect, I was watching a video clip of a short sermon excerpt someone sent to me. The person who sent it to me thought it was hot stuff. In this clip, a nationally known television preacher was whooping it up, preaching and hollering something about the need for people to press through their tired state. Many in this large congregation were standing up and wagging their heads and waving their hands, but, all the while, I was sensing *grief.*

Trying hard not to be critical, I pondered what I was watching. "Why am I sensing this grief, Lord? What is this? It feels so unclean to me." As I continued to weigh the heaviness in my spirit, here are the words I heard:

"It's just a show — you're sensing the showmanship and the love of appearance that is such a big part of Christianity in the West today. It is as little children 'playing church.' It is a subtle religious form of man-centered entertainment. But because Scripture is attached to it, people are often deceived by it and don't realize that they are receiving another spirit."

More of my own questions raced through my mind: "Do you sense His presence at all? Can you relate even a little to these people's excitement? What do you think will happen to these people? What is at the root of this sort of behavior?"

Honest responses rose up within me: "There is no *presence of God* here. I sense nothing. It is only emotion. I feel so disconnected from these people's excitement. Most of them have made a huge idol out of this celebrity preacher, and whatever he says, they will receive it as Bible. He is not leading them to you, Lord."

I continued to muse within myself: "It seems to me that these people are being further and further separated from your holy knowledge. Unless they have a rude awakening, they will never really know you and your ways, will they Lord? What will be their end?"

The truth seems to be that they have formed another god — according to their own brand of Christianity. It's almost as if Christianity has been separated from Christ Himself. That is a very sobering thought that reveals volumes about Christianity in many places.

The curse of Christianity today in much of the West may well be the creation of an image of God that is according to the religious culture people find themselves in. We have the Charismatic culture, the Evangelical culture, the new Catholic culture, the Baptist culture, etc. We have the prophetic camp, the word of faith camp, the vineyard camp, the revival camp, and on and on. Infiltrated into many of these cultures and camps is the seeker-friendly philosophy of reaching larger numbers of people, based on a removal or a veiling of Christian theology that is least appealing to the world. But for the most part, in the visible-to-the-eye mainstream of Christianity, except perhaps in a few places, the Lord is not being glorified because we are so divided.

People don't need a cultural Jesus or a traditional Jesus or a seeker-friendly Jesus. They need a Living Word that will pierce through the veil of their own hearts and reveal the real Jesus to them. They need an encounter with the true glory of God.

The love of appearance is killing us spiritually. I'm not speaking of "appearance" as having things *look* honorable and excellent, but something else. The root of this stronghold that I call "love of appearance" is not outward. I'm speaking of something much more deceptive. It is superficiality — an irreverence, a pride and hypocrisy that was unknown in the early Church. Ananias and Sapphira walked in it and were struck down. They wanted to be recognized for their generosity and having given all, so, for the love of appearance, they lied, and then they died. It was more spiritual than physical — inward, not outward.

No one but the Holy Spirit knew what was going on in their hearts. One of the greatest needs of the hour is for more prophets and apostles like Peter, full of the Holy Spirit, who are able to see right through man-made façades and then preach a burning word that convicts of sin and cuts away motives, attitudes, and things that are dishonoring to God. We need the mighty, piercing anointing of the Spirit to turn our hearts completely and unreservedly toward God.

During this time, the early Church was yet in its infancy. They were still localized in Jerusalem only. If this pride and hypocrisy, rooted in the love of appearance, had been allowed to fester and grow, it would've marred the purity of Christ's body and killed the glory. Instead, the glory killed the pride and hypocrisy that Ananias and

Sapphira entertained.

The lesson we learn here is that the level of judgment is always equal to the level of glory.

During my viewing of the aforementioned video clip, I caught another all-too-familiar glimpse of the self-based nature of the modern gospel and the mainstream word that is preached. Nothing of Christ, the Holy Spirit, or anything bearing His character and nature was mentioned.

Like far too many messages today, it was all about us. It was all about us overcoming, us fighting, us getting our blessing, us receiving all that is ours, with no focus or even minor referencing to Jesus and His heart and ways. As I wrote in my book, *The Real Gospel*, this all points to an inordinate deification of man that has become the apex of 21st-century Christianity in America whereby millions of people are being deceived.

I believe the only way the glory can be restored in the Church today is through humility, true repentance, and the fear of the Lord. We must fall to our knees and repent of the vanity and futility of our own efforts. Large crowds and man's approval are not sure-proof signs of a move of God or that preachers even know Him.

I say this with pain in my heart, but much of the ungodliness in present-day America falls on the shoulders of preachers. We've led people to us and to our visions, ministries, and churches more than to Him. We've exalted charisma, talent, attendance, buildings, cash, religious activity, and the love of appearance far more than we have the Holy One.

Ananias and Sapphira stood before Peter clutching on to a lie based on a desire to be recognized and esteemed, rooted in the love of appearance. Unbeknownst to them, however, was the fact that they stood not before man, but before the high court of heaven and the majestic glory of Him whom John, when he saw Him, *"fell at his feet as dead"* (Rev. 1:17).

Are our lives and corporate gatherings marked with this holy focus and awareness of Him whose glory no flesh can stand?

Jesus is walking amidst the lampstands, which represent the churches (Rev. 2:1). He is not as concerned with the government, the economy, or world affairs as He is with His churches.

Can we see Him, or is all the smoke from the methods and machinery of men blocking our view?

CHAPTER 5

CHRISTIAN TOTEMISM:

MAKING JESUS WHAT YOU WANT HIM TO BE

All these things Jesus spoke to the multitude in parables; and without a parable He did not speak to them, that it might be fulfilled which was spoken by the prophet, saying: "I will open My mouth in parables; I will utter things kept secret from the foundation of the world" (Mt. 13:34-35).

The deep thoughts of God were always revealed through Jesus, the wisdom of God, as He spoke in parables things hidden from the foundation of the world.

Jesus spoke in parables because the mystery of God could not be revealed to the multitudes. Those who desired to understand those mysteries would draw closer to Jesus in a more private setting (v 36). This way, the insincere and the curiosity crowd could be divided from the true seekers.

The spoken wisdom of God embodied in Jesus was like a sword that cut away the fat that made people's ears heavy and dull. The sword of His word circumcised them to hear and receive truth. Those who yielded to this sword were separated from the popular camp of the scribes and Pharisees, and others who served religious systems that made mention of God but who didn't have a true revelation of Him.

Too many in our church pulpits have taken a moratorium on Christ's identity. The popular, politically correct, and "wannabe" culturally relevant American church is saying of Jesus Christ: "You are the one who makes us feel good. You are the one who understands our sinful issues and addictions. You are the one who blesses us and makes us rich." Some of that is actually true. He does understand, and He does bless, but the image portrayed of a pie-in-the-sky type of god makes the spirit of it false. He cannot be whatever we want or need Him to be.

"It is quite an education when I consider the degree of anger and hostility I get from "Christians" when I simply point out the ethics that Jesus taught, you know, 'red letter' stuff, like, love your enemies, do good to them who spitefully use you, etc. People will dodge, dance, resist, resent, fight, attack, slander, and any number of other lovely "Christian" behaviors for the right to cling to retributive justice and other unbiblical and ungodly beliefs, especially when Jesus' ethics challenge their own. Once when dealing with an elder's wife on an issue, I pointed to what Jesus said (in context, properly exegeted), in her own "red letter" Bible, that was contrary to what she was believing, clinging to, and fighting me about. Her exact words to me: 'My Jesus is not like that.' Precisely, that is the problem."

Dr. Stephen Crosby

The Church presents Christ as the therapist, the banker, the philosopher, the friend, the hippie, the social activist, the look-the-other-way zero-accountability spiritual figure.

Why are the majority of people in the West so confused or deceived about who Jesus really is? Why do they seem to have so little depth or spiritual substance in their lives? Why can't these people's Christianity go beyond, "Jesus said, 'do not judge'?" Is it not in large part due to the distorted message of Him that our pulpits, our preachers, and our churches are presenting? Is it not for the lack of example we've had in many Christian leaders? Similarly, the reason for much of today's current moral and cultural malaise stems from the Church's distorted message of the Christ.

The image of Jesus for many professing Christians has been shaped by the society around them. Unless you have an intimate relationship with the Holy One and His Word, the image you have of Him will be distorted. It will resemble the pop culture you live in and what the people of that culture worship. In the West, self is god.

Corruptible man is worshipped. Humanism rules. And this is what we see in much of today's Church.

If a professing believer does not want to give up his carnal, sinful lifestyle and adhere to the Lord's ways, he can just create an image of God that makes room for his sinful lifestyle. It is a very subtle deception that comforts and consoles him in his carnality and sin by saying things like, "God knows my heart," or "God understands my struggles." These types of comments, however, are usually made as a way of defending his lifestyle and justifying his carnal appetites. Is the Jesus you serve a product of your own desires patterned after this world, or is He the true presence of the Living Word of God in your life?

For example, divorce is now a rampant part of our Western culture, and the divorce rate in the church is nearly equal to that in the world. Many professing Christians find an unscriptural excuse to leave their spouses, and, in contradiction to the will of God, they forsake the vows they once made. And now that our culture is deteriorating to levels of sexual anarchy, professing Christians are claiming that one can also be gay and be a Christian. This is what happens when professing Christians flow with the spirit of the world. The image of God in them changes.

Emil Durkheim, the classic father of sociology, wrote extensively about totemism. Totemism is derived from the word "totem," which is a natural object or an animate being, such as an animal or bird, assumed to be the emblem of a clan, family, or group. It can be an object or a natural phenomenon that a family considers itself to be closely related to; a totem serves as a distinctive mark of that group or family. Totemism is the belief in the kinship of groups or individuals having a common totem and the rituals, taboos, and practices associated with such a belief.

Durkheim described totemism as the human tendency to form a conception of God in our own image. He said that oftentimes human beings, whether they are jungle tribes or sophisticated city dwellers, will take the values and traditions that they admire most about themselves and project them onto a totem. Eventually, they stand in awe of that totem and end up worshipping an incarnation of the things they love about themselves. This is what people do with the image of God. We create an image of a god whom we can relate to and who cares about the same things we care about.

During the days of Moses, Israel was living in an environment that worshipped images of animals and creeping things, and so a golden calf was fashioned from the people's gold and worshipped (Ex. 32). *"Professing to be wise, they became fools, and changed the glory of the incorruptible God into an image made like corruptible man — and birds and four-footed animals and creeping things"* (Rom. 1:22-23). Their culture influenced and shaped their image of God. If you don't stay in God's presence and in God's Word, the same thing could happen to you.

Beware of idolatry and changing the image of an incorruptible God into corruptible man.

In the West, worshipping golden images of animals and insects is not as prominent. As I stated, we worship something more subtle: self.

The fewer preconceptions we bring from the outside to the reading of the gospels, the more clearly we shall see Him as He really is. It is all too easy to believe in a Jesus who is largely a construction of our own imagination — an inoffensive Person whom no one could dislike or disapprove of, and certainly whom no one would ever crucify.

But the Jesus we meet in the gospels is far from being an inoffensive person. On the contrary, He caused offense quite frequently. Even His loyal followers found Him to be offensive at times, even disconcerting. He upset all established notions of religious propriety.

An inaccurate, distorted, and unbiblical view of Jesus is a big reason why many pastors fail to confront sin in the Church and speak of the evils in our society.

When asked why pastors don't speak out against the evils in our nation and government, one influential pastor said, *"I think one reason is a lot of Christian leaders have the wrong idea about Jesus. They see Jesus as this little, wimpy guy who walked around plucking daisies and eating birdseed and saying nice things, but never doing anything controversial."*

"The fact is, Jesus did confront his culture with truth — and he ended up being crucified because of it. I believe it's time for pastors to say, 'You know, I don't care about controversy, I don't care whether I'm going to lose church members, I don't care about building a big church. I'm going to stand for truth, regardless of what happens.'"

At times, the greatest love we can demonstrate is in rebuke. Conversely, at times, the greatest cruelty we can demonstrate is in never confronting sin or evil.

"Nothing can be more cruel than the tenderness that consigns another to their sin. Nothing can be more compassionate than the severe rebuke that calls a brother back from the path of sin." Dietrich Bonhoeffer

Jesus said what He meant and meant what He said. If you read His words assuming otherwise, then you are not encountering the real Jesus.

The rich, powerful, and famous have the eyes of everyone. For the most part, you won't see Jesus there. To see Jesus, look for Him among the poor, the powerless, and the obscure — all the people that the world ignores, or worse.

The Church, with all its faults and flaws, is the body of Christ. *"Wherever two or three are gathered together in My name, there I am in the midst of them."* If you want to see the real Jesus, look for him among the humble gatherings of your pure-hearted brothers and sisters in Christ. Open your eyes to see Him. He is there.

CHAPTER 6

GOD (JESUS) IS LOVE, GOD (JESUS) IS HOLY:

RESTORING THE BALANCE OF LOVE AND HOLINESS

The words of R.C. Sproul ring so true in this hour.

"Holiness provokes hatred. The greater the holiness, the greater the human hostility toward it. It seems insane. No man was ever more loving than Jesus Christ. Yet even His love made people angry. His love was a perfect love, a transcendent and holy love, but His very love brought trauma to people. This kind of love is so majestic we can't stand it." (R.C. Sproul, *The Holiness of God*)

Holiness is not love, and love is not holiness, but there is a love that is holy.

Years ago, I was preaching a series of strong holiness messages in a particular church. After one of the meetings, the pastor said something to me that I've never forgotten. "The Lord has dealt with me about preaching more on love than on holiness," he said.

That statement didn't sit well with me. I knew it was not accurate. Yet, back then, I didn't know why. I pondered that pastor's statement with my own thoughts that raced through my head. Is love more important than holiness? Are they different, or are they virtually the same? *They have to be different, or we'd have a lot of redundancy in the Bible,* I thought. But how are they different? Although I knew the pastor's statement came from a lack of understanding true holiness, at that time, I couldn't thoroughly explain the difference.

This pastor's statement put an emphasis on love, which is of primary importance, while de-emphasizing holiness, which is not only God's greatest attribute but foundational to understanding man's relationship to God. I walked away from that conversation knowing that this pastor's view of holiness was not becoming or beautiful. I thought of how his view was probably shared by a multitude of believers who have formed erroneous ideas and notions about holiness, due probably to their own negative experiences — like the cat who is afraid of water because of one negative experience of getting scalded by boiling water. Or of those who may have come from a background of legalism, where do's and don'ts were associated with holiness. These are among the reasons holiness has gotten such a bad rap and is looked upon with a sort of disdain, as being primitive, outdated, and just not culturally relevant. We need to realize, however, that negative experiences or unsound teaching does not nullify the real meaning, necessity, and beauty of God's holiness.

What, then, is the real meaning of holiness? Holiness is the likeness of God. It is the total summation of all His attributes. One of my favorite definitions of holiness as it applies to believers is that it is a moral dedication and a life committed to purity of thought, word, motive, and deed. At the center of that definition is the fact of being set apart or consecrated to God's purposes. Just as God is otherworldly, we, as His chosen people, are to be distinct and set apart from this world. In other words, we are not to be conformed to its ideals, patterns, or standards. Holiness is conformity to God's nature and will.

But even more importantly, holiness has more to do with whom we belong to. To whom do we give our loyalty, love, and allegiance? To be holy means that all we are and all we have belongs to God, not ourselves, and is set apart for His purposes. It means that every aspect of our lives is to be shaped and directed by God, which is a continual process in our lives, called *sanctification*. Walking in holiness of heart causes every component of our character to stand God's inspection and meet His approval.

Personally, I believe that restoring the beauty of biblical holiness in the Church is a critical ingredient to healing the moral confusion in our culture. As the Church goes, so goes the world. Our disproportionate view of holiness is one of the big reasons there is so much of the spirit of the world in the Church. A distorted view of holiness, or simply the ignorance of it, is clouding our understanding of God's true love. When God is seen as a loving, non-demanding pushover whose love overrides His holiness, then people will live in accordance with that belief. Permissiveness and promiscuity will be prevalent.

For example, if a person believes God is so loving that He would never allow anyone to go to hell for his sin, then his conduct will reflect that belief, and much of his life will be lived with that awful presumption. Popular-but-false concepts of God such as these are rampant in much of Western culture. A vision and revelation of God's holiness will alter any of these false perceptions and will serve to greatly strengthen the Church.

Any understanding of sin must begin with an understanding of true Biblical holiness. In Canaan, the temple prostitute was considered a holy woman, and a homosexual priest was considered a holy man. However, what was accepted among the Canaanites and the other nations was an abomination to God (Dt. 23:17-18). And Israel, as God's chosen nation, a type of the New Testament Church, was forbidden to practice these things. The people of Canaan didn't understand God's holiness so they couldn't possibly understand the gravity of their sin.

A person defines sin by his own concept of God. As I've already mentioned, this is the reason we now have books being written that one can be a homosexual Christian; and now we also have the spread of universalism and the emergent church that teaches that, in the end, all will be saved, because God will not allow any human being to go to hell. Many do not understand God's love because they are not seeing it through His holiness.

Our understanding of God's holiness determines our estimation of sin. God defines Himself through His holiness. His holiness is the standard by which we judge what sin is and what sin is not. Righteousness and justice, which are vital aspects of God's holiness, are the foundation of His throne (Ps. 89:14). All God's dealings with us are based on the foundation of holiness. *"Nevertheless the solid foundation of God stands, having this seal: 'The Lord knows those who are His,' and, 'Let everyone who names the name of Christ depart from iniquity'"* (2 Tim. 2:19).

It is wrong to elevate what we think is love at the expense of holiness. In fact, God's true love manifests within holiness. Just as water flows through a pipe, the love of God flows through His holiness. Moreover, it is God's love that keeps Him from overlooking His holiness. After all, it was His holiness that made the atonement necessary. His holiness demanded the cost of God's own Son, for He cannot excuse, acquit, or clear the guilty (Ex. 34:7). And what His holiness demanded, His love provided on the cross of Calvary.

Holiness and love are not at odds with each other. Holiness is not in opposition to love or separated from it. The Bible tells us that love is the greatest of all graces (1 Cor. 13:13) and any word, motivation, or act void of love is as nothing (1 Cor. 13:1-3). But at the same time, love is not separated from holiness, for we cannot see God without it. *"Pursue peace with all people, and holiness, without which no one will see the Lord"* (Heb. 12:14). Rather, love is constrained by holiness.

For example, if a church will not draw a sharp distinction between sin and righteousness, or will not practice church discipline among its members as taught in the Word (Mt. 18:15-17, Rom. 16:17, 1 Cor. 5, Tit. 3:10, 2 Thes. 3:6, 14-15, etc.) because it doesn't seem loving, it has probably been deceived into a false view of love absorbed from the pop culture and a lukewarm church. On the other hand, a church that emphasizes holiness, yet fails to do so in the motivation and service of love, is a church that does not understand God's holiness.

The true love of God is fixed on God's holiness. If a church does not abide in true holiness, it does not abide in true love. Conversely, if it does not abide in true love, it does not abide in true holiness.

If we don't feel a sense of awe and fear or reverence for the beauty of God's holiness, which opposes all wickedness and evil with wrath and fury, we cannot possibly understand God's true character in relation to man and the world.

A holy church is *in* the world but not *of* it. They abstain from sin while dwelling among sinners — both are characteristics of true holiness. The problem has been that some churches have swerved too far in one direction or too far in the other, waffling between a false view of holiness and a false view of love.

Tell me if this sounds like the real Jesus:

Did Jesus speak out against the unjust practices of the tax collectors?

Not really. Instead He had dinner with them and befriended them.

Did Jesus lead a massive march for the inclusion of women and Gentiles in the Jewish world?

No, He simply included them in His "world."

Did Jesus lead a huge movement against the violent practices of the Zealots?

Once again, no. He befriended them.

Did Jesus ever protest against the oppressive practices of the Roman Empire?

No, but He did ease the suffering of their centurions by healing those dear to them.

Do you ever remember Jesus leading a movement to rid Jerusalem's streets of immorality?

I don't. Instead, He welcomed the prostitutes and sinners.

Did Jesus ever take to the streets against the governing authorities for their lack of concern for the poor, sick, and outcasts?

No, He fed them, healed them, and focused His ministry on them.

The root sickness of the world is not cured by placing standards upon it. The sickness of the world is cured when we become the standard of love. (Courtesy of Loren Rosser)

The same Bible that tells us to pursue holiness (Heb. 12:14) tells us to pursue love (1 Cor. 14:1). Without holiness, we will never see the Lord. But without love, we are nothing.

It's time for the modern-day Church to get that right and walk in that light.

CHAPTER 7

JESUS LOVES, JESUS HATES:

YOU CAN'T TRULY LOVE UNLESS YOU HATE

Just as there needs to be a balance between love and holiness, so there must be a balanced understanding of love and hate. This is especially true in the cultural war of "gay rights."

One major cause of the gay community's madness, and even the displeasure of some professing Christians toward Biblically sound views of homosexuality, is what they perceive as a lack of love in addressing and even accepting this sinful behavior. There is this smug arrogance among some people today, many of whom are half my age or younger, who claim to be such experts in love. Ironically, it's these same proponents of love who vehemently curse and ridicule those who are outspoken in expressing Biblical views of homosexuality.

Human love is so fickle. This natural kind of conditional love is always based on what it can get. It loves only those who love them. But God's love is unconditional. He loved us and died for us while we were yet sinners (Rom. 5:8). He loves sinners today. He loves homosexuals, even those who stick their nose up at Him and defame His name. It is His infinite mercy and long-suffering, along with His desire that none perish, that allow Him to wait for repentance (2 Pt. 3:9).

People, even good Christian folks, forget that the same Jesus who loves all mankind and is moved with compassion is also the One who rebukes sin, pride, and hypocrisy, and speaks the truth without compromise. He laid down many judgments in the Scriptures upon those who rejected Him and who refused to come to repentance and obedience.

Let us not forget that it was Jesus who said, *"He who does not believe will be condemned"* (Mk. 16:16). Does that sound like love? How can a loving God let people be condemned? They reject His words.

He also said this: *"Unless you repent you will all likewise perish"* (Lk. 13:3). Does that sound like love? Again, would a compassionate God let people perish? If they do not repent, yes. What do people need to repent of? Sin and all that is displeasing to God and in opposition to His moral laws. Homosexuality is on that list.

Jesus healed a crippled man and then told him: *"Sin no more, lest a worse thing come upon you"* (Jn. 5:14).

Jesus showed mercy to the adulterous woman only after she was ridden with guilt and broken. He will also show mercy to every homosexual who humbles himself in true contrition and acknowledges his sin with a desire to be free. After Jesus showed the adulterous woman mercy and released her from her condemnation, He also commanded her to go and sin no more (Jn. 8:11). This is a wonderful example of grace and law, and mercy and truth working together.

Jesus also displayed anger and pronounced judgments on individuals, groups of people, and nations, even calling them names.

Here are some examples. *"Woe unto you scribes and Pharisees, hypocrites, blind guides, fools and blind, serpents and generation of vipers (snakes)!"* (Mt. 23). That's a lot of name calling right there. Sounds like what people call "hate" today.

In fact, it would do us all good to read Jesus' judgments upon a wicked and perverse generation in Matthew 23 to set aright our own image of Jesus. His love was not this sentimental, mushy kind of philosophical love that has no hatred for unrighteousness and wickedness. Yes, He is love, but He is also just and holy. Yes, he is merciful, but He is also faithful and true in establishing His judgments.

When we read the Scripture through the lens of psychotherapeutic values of "not hurting others' feelings" and cultural sensibilities of what is "nice" and "kind" and "polite," we construct an idolatrous image of God based, again, on how we think and act.

We tend to forget, in this fickle world of ours, that some of the greatest prophets were men who called people to repentance and challenged them to turn to God. And very often, they didn't mince words. For example, John the Baptist publicly rebuked Herod, the tetrarch, for his adultery with his brother's wife (Lk. 3:19). His penalty: Prison and then beheading. His crime? Calling out sin. Sounds like "hate" to modern-day spiritual pacifists.

Truth sounds like hate to those who hate the truth.

What about the following New Testament verses? Notice the directness of these verses I've already made reference to and how different kinds of sinful behavior are identified and called out.

"Do you not know that the unrighteous will not inherit the kingdom of God? Do not be deceived. Neither fornicators, nor idolaters, nor adulterers, nor homosexuals, nor sodomites, nor thieves, nor covetous, nor drunkards, nor revilers, nor extortioners will inherit the kingdom of God" (1 Cor. 6:9-10).

How do you get around these verses? Note the references to sexual immorality. Fornicators, adulterers, homosexuals, and sodomites will not inherit the kingdom of God.

How about this one written to believers?

"But fornication and all uncleanness (includes homosexuality) *or covetousness, let it not even be named among you, as is fitting for saints...For this you know, that no fornicator, unclean person* (that would include homosexuality), *nor covetous man, who is an idolater, has any inheritance in the kingdom of Christ and God"* (Eph. 5:3, 5).

It would behoove some of us to read those verses very slowly.

But here's the good news. All sinners can change, even homosexuals, just as many of the Corinthians were changed by the power of God.

"And such were some of you. But you were washed, but you were sanctified, but you were justified in the name of the Lord Jesus and by the Spirit of our God" (1 Cor. 6:11).

Here's my concern.

The love of many believers seems to be waxing cold because of their desire not to offend anyone but to be accepted by all (Mt. 24:12). This false concept of love as a sentiment of total acceptance, free of the ability to hate, is one of the most popular rationales for which many believers are abandoning the truth and authority of the Scriptures in this hour.

Loving people is certainly a godly virtue, but not at the expense of hating or forsaking truth and righteousness. I'm afraid that the modern definition of love in much of the Church is "being nice." But "being nice" is not necessarily love. In reality, this could very well be the shallowest form of love, as well as the most deceptive and dangerous.

The Church is so ill-advised in this matter of true love that we will actually damn people's souls to hell because we're too "nice" to tell them the truth that could save their souls. True love is willing to go far beyond only being nice, and embrace righteousness and be hated and rejected for speaking the truth.

The big problem is that we are not familiar with the Biblical Jesus. Too many Christians want a manageable, domesticated Jesus who makes no demands on their time, money, words, social life, or sexuality, but is just nice. In the midst of this great and growing deception, God is looking for uncompromising believers who are full of true love but are also committed to proclaiming the truth that is in Jesus, and not the counterfeit Jesus of Western culture. Too many professing Christians don't know the real Jesus but are just following the Jesus of the pop culture — the one who shallow and naive Christians have made Him to be.

Loving people is certainly a godly virtue and the most important of all commandments. We need to be measured in pursuing love, and we can "be nice" while doing it but not at the expense of hating or compromising truth and betraying righteousness. The focus of what many call "love" today is based on accommodating people's ungodly and sinful lifestyles and idiosyncrasies, and frankly, even abominable behavior.

Jesus Christ loved righteousness and hated iniquity or evil (Heb. 1:8-9). A love for God and His righteousness is the foundation of true love. But it is impossible to love God's righteousness without *hating* wickedness. No true love can tolerate wickedness. To act indifferent toward wickedness and evil is proof of an absence of a love for righteousness in your life. No morality that fails to hate wickedness has ever known righteousness.

Understand that hate, in itself, is not sin. It all depends on what you hate. Hating wickedness is an attribute of God and, therefore, a godly virtue. Hating righteousness, however, is sin. Hating those who love righteousness is sin. Hating your brother is sin, for it is equated with murder (1 Jn. 3:15). Hating God is, of course, sin.

Human love, which is sympathetic, if not balanced with a hatred for evil and a true love for righteousness, disqualifies the Christian for battle in this cultural war. As I stated, here in America and much of the West, we are in the midst of a huge cultural war and a moral crisis, with homosexuality and gay rights at the center of it, but the greater threat to society and the Church could be this false concept of love.

The perfect balance of love and hate can function only in Jesus Christ and those who are truly His. God's love is capable of loving sinners without condoning sin. Even we who have children know to love them but also to hate the evils that could damage them.

This is why I hate lying, thievery, murder, rape, adultery, fornication, and homosexuality — because they are evil.

Just as pain is necessary to alert us of danger in our bodies, so is hate a necessary companion to true love.

Jesus loves and Jesus hates. Let us do the same.

FEAR OF REJECTION AND PERSECUTION

This disturbing trend among many Christians today to remain silent concerning the very important moral and cultural issues of our time is hurting the cause of Christianity. In surveying these Christians, I have found that their refusal to provide a clear witness of the gospel boils down to one thing: They fear rejection and persecution. They fear being classified as hateful, bigoted, homophobic, and nasty evangelical idiots.

There is no question we must demonstrate love in presenting the true gospel, especially when we confront the sins of our culture, but my concern is in how we've misunderstood the expressions of love and hate. In order to truly love something, you must hate something else. I love righteousness, therefore, I hate sin and wickedness. I love life, therefore, I hate death. I love health and healing, therefore, I hate sickness and disease. I love Jesus Christ, therefore, I hate Satan. I love traditional marriage as God designed it, therefore, I hate gay/same-sex marriage.

There is such a militant aggression in our society today that is demanding that people love and accept others. This new sentiment is shaping public policy and being used as a standard of morality in evaluating people's behavior. Even many Christians are falling for it, and demonic doctrines and damnable heresies are spreading.

I was recently reading the reviews of one of Dr. Dobson's books on rearing children. I was shocked at how many so-called Christians were highly critical of his conservative stance on homosexuality and other issues of our times. Here is a small sample of them:

"Those extremists have no respect from me, and I refuse to be a part of their hate based on some preacher's interpretation of the Bible. I will attend only inclusive churches from now on. I'm taking a stand for equality and love. I'll choose that over hate and bullying any day."

"There are lots of words I'd use to describe this book and its

author, but 'practical' is not one of them. Some words I would use would include: 'bigoted,' 'homophobic,' 'insane,' 'illogical,' 'silly,' 'sexist,' 'Nazi-ish,' and 'stupid.'"

"This book is so offensive and filled with such hate...."

After reading many such reviews, I realized that most of these readers were particularly offended by one chapter opposing homosexuality, which was based on the scriptures. And these critics were not gay. They were family people, in traditional marriages, interested in learning to raise children.

We are living in a day of which the prophet Isaiah spoke: "*So truth fails, and he who departs from evil makes himself a prey*" (Is. 59:14).

One definition of prey is a person or thing that becomes the victim of a hostile person, influence, etc. True Christians will be increasingly victimized by a humanistic culture that deifies man and opposes God's righteousness and truth. One who stands for God's righteousness and truth in this hour will be persecuted and hated, and some may even be killed, right here in America. Don't worry or be fearful, because we are in great company, for, as I stated earlier, Jesus Christ Himself loved righteousness and hated iniquity (evil). He was a perfect Man, and they killed Him.

This godless philosophy that claims a love, respect, and tolerance for everyone without the ability to hate anything is paralyzing many professing Christians from rising up and standing against evil. People have become so objective that they can't even be stirred to anger against the gross evils that have permeated our society. These are characteristics of a people whom the Bible speaks of as, "*ever learning but never coming to the knowledge of the truth*" (2 Tim. 3:7).

CHAPTER 8

THE MAJESTY AND CONDESCENSION OF JESUS

There I was on one of Atlanta's superhighways. stuck in bumper-to-bumper rush-hour traffic. I was allowing myself to get frustrated as my wife tried to assure me that eventually the traffic would break up and we would move. "There's nothing we can do. Being frustrated is not going to help the situation!" she exclaimed, adding, "Why don't you just praise the Lord?" Thank God for sensible and virtuous wives!

After finally letting my hasty emotions subside, I began to meditate on the Lord and receive His peace. Then I started thinking about the Father's love and care, and recounting how good He'd been to me and my family. Specifically, a vision a minister friend of mine had of the Father's unconditional love was floating in my thoughts.

In this vision, my friend was somewhere in the Middle East about three feet off the ground. He was observing a Muslim couple praying to Allah to meet their needs. The husband needed to sell his vegetables in the marketplace so that his wife could purchase a mirror, a hairbrush, and one other item, and I believe their rent was also due. They asked Allah for these things, and then the man put his vegetables on his cart and headed out to the market.

Before he even got to the market, a man came running to him and requested to buy all his vegetables. With restrained excitement, the man gladly sold him all his vegetables and ran home to tell his wife how Allah had prospered his day. They both rejoiced and gave thanks.

In this vision, the heavenly Father then told my friend, "I did that for them."

My friend responded, "But Father, they are Muslims, and they prayed to Allah, a false god."

"Haven't you read in my word where I cause the sun to rise on the evil and on the good, and I send rain on the just and on the unjust?"

"You have heard that it was said, 'You shall love your neighbor and hate your enemy.' But I say to you, love your enemies, bless those who curse you, do good to those who hate you, and pray for those who spitefully use you and persecute you, that you may be sons of your Father in heaven; **for He makes His sun rise on the evil and on the good, and sends rain on the just and on the unjust"** (Mt. 5:43-45).

At first, this vision my friend had messed with my theology just as it did his. But when this scripture was given to him by the Spirit of God, I accepted it, and I received more light concerning the goodness and kindness of our loving Father.

God is righteous, holy, and just, but He is also very kind, merciful, and full of compassion. That is the part of His character that is most appealing and most attractive to mankind. It inspires faith and praise in us and pulls on our heart-strings.

Read the following verse very slowly, and let it be engraved in your heart forever.

"The Lord is gracious and full of compassion, slow to anger and great in mercy. The Lord is good to all, and His tender mercies are over all His works" (Ps. 145:8-9).

As I was reflecting on the thoughts of the aforementioned vision, my heart began to rejoice in the beauty and lovingkindness of the Lord. Stuck in the middle of rush-hour traffic, suddenly a song came forth from my heart to the Lord:

"I love the way You are

Lord, I love the way You are,

I love, I love the way You are.

Your heart, it captivates me,

Your beauty fascinates me,

And I love, I love the way You are."

I sang this little melody over and over again, with tears of gratitude and then with joy and laughter interspersed throughout this time of loving and adoring the Lord. Needless to say, I forgot all about the rush-hour traffic as I was filled with the Spirit.

Just a glimpse of the Lord's beauty, kindness, and compassion will melt your heart. A revelation of His love and grace is the transforming power of every life.

HIS FIRST APPEARANCE SPEAKS VOLUMES ABOUT HIS NATURE

After the resurrection, Jesus appeared first to a woman named Mary Magdalene.

"Now when He rose early on the first day of the week, He appeared first to Mary Magdalene, out of whom He had cast seven demons" (Mk. 16:9).

Think of it. During one of the greatest moments in the history of mankind, Jesus chose to visit a former promiscuous woman of ill repute — one who has the Biblical distinction of having had seven devils cast out of her by Jesus (Lk. 8:2). She may have even been a street dweller who had spent her time gathering scraps of old, stale food from garbage heaps. The resurrected Jesus didn't visit the king, or the prime minister, or some VIP or dignitary to announce His resurrection. That is what a mere man would've done. That is what the wisdom of man would've dictated. But not Jesus. He is other-worldly.

Jesus chose *not* to appear to the mighty, the noble, and the wise according to the flesh, but instead He chose to appear to the foolish, the weak, the base, and the despised of this world (1 Cor. 1:26-29). That's just the way He is, so that no flesh can glory in His presence.

At the empty tomb, the angel also delivered a special announcement and message for Jesus' disciples, especially Peter.

"But go, tell His disciples — and Peter — that He is going before

you into Galilee; there you will see Him, as He said to you" (Mk. 16:7).

Why did the angel single out Peter? Wasn't it because Peter had wept bitterly when he denied Jesus before three different people (Lk. 22:62). Jesus wanted him to know, that although he'd failed Him and denied Him, he was forgiven because Jesus had overcome sin, death, and the grave.

Peter was in a low place, broken-hearted and full of regret, and that is where Jesus met him. Such is the meekness of Christ. He seeks out the lowly. He heals the broken-hearted. He comforts the afflicted. He exalts the humble. He defends the widow. He's a Father to the fatherless and the orphan. That is our majestic God! He is a God of condescension.

Think of the virgin Mary, the teenage girl chosen to be the mother of Jesus. She was a lowly peasant girl and certainly unqualified to be the mother of the Son of God. But it is the unqualified whom God often chooses because they qualify for the impossible to be done. The unqualified do not have a high assessment of their own status or ability because their confidence is in the mighty God.

Mary knew who she was: *"For He has regarded the lowly state of His maidservant ..."* (Lk. 1:48). Likewise, she also knew who was calling her to birth the impossible.

"For He who is mighty has done great things for me..." (Lk. 1:49).

Behold the majesty and condescension of our loving and merciful God!

"The Lord is high above all nations, His glory above the heavens.

Who is like the Lord our God, Who dwells on high, Who humbles Himself to behold the things that are in the heavens and in the earth? He raises the poor out of the dust, and lifts the needy out of the ash heap, that He may seat him with princes — with the princes of His people. He grants the barren woman a home, like a joyful mother of children" (Ps. 113:4-9).

Think of the many characters God used throughout the Bible, — even in the Old Testament. Most of them were lowly and unqualified. Time will not permit me to write of Moses, Gideon, David, Jeremiah and others who had to deal with an inferiority complex to even obey God and place their confidence in Him.

Although the Lord is highly exalted and perfectly holy, He is drawn to that which is lowly. He is drawn to that which is broken. He is drawn to the humble and contrite heart.

"The Lord is near to those who have a broken heart, and saves such as have a contrite spirit" (Ps. 34:18).

"For thus says the High and Lofty One who inhabits eternity, whose name is Holy: 'I dwell in the high and holy place, with him who has a contrite and humble spirit, to revive the spirit of the humble, and to revive the heart of the contrite ones'" (Is. 57:15).

"Heaven is My throne, and earth is My footstool. Where is the house that you will build Me? And where is the place of My rest? For all those things My hand has made, and all those things exist," says the Lord. *"But on this one will I look: On him who is poor and of a contrite spirit, and who trembles at My word"* (Is. 66:1-2).

The Lord delights in revealing Himself to him who is lowly, humble, poor, and contrite. Just as water flows to the lowest level, even so the Lord's mercy and compassion flows to the lowest of humanity.

Mere men want to be grand and arrogant and proud and in control and full of something they assume to be God's power. But then again, the Scripture tells us that no flesh will glory in His presence.

Broken people, poor people, needy people, as well as those without all the answers don't appeal to our sense of pomp and pageantry, of greatness and grandeur. In fact, they often offend us. Transparent people who have grown tired of hiding their warts from a holy God, those who are naked, raw, and undignified in their disposition — those weary of trying to be somebody else and hiding behind a false, projected image are usually despised and rejected by those who still love to save face and maintain reputation.

The Lord is other-worldly and does not think and act like mere man. He is not impressed by our impressions. He is not persuaded by our projections. He is not moved with what often moves us. He resists the proud but gives grace to the humble (Jam. 4:6). Humility is what moves the Lord. Brokenness is what touches His heart.

The Lord is *moved* with compassion because He is *full* of compassion. You are moved by what you're full of. When you are full of something, there is no room for anything else. Throughout the earthly ministry of Jesus, you will find that He was continually moved with compassion to heal the sick and needy (Mt. 14:13-14) (Mk. 1:41). He did not heal the sick and do miracles so He could prove His deity, but because of His desire to reveal the Father's heart and compassion and willingness to help, heal, and deliver. Because Jesus was the express will of God in action, He was demonstrating the merciful and compassionate character of God the Father. After all, God is called the Father of mercies (2 Cor. 1:3).

That characteristic is what inspires us to have faith and believe God for healing or any other benefit or answer to prayer that you know is the will of God.

Compassion and mercy are the same root word in the Greek language. Compassion means to love tenderly, to pity, to show mercy, and to be full of eager yearning. Oh, how I love to meditate on that definition! It reveals the depth of the greatest attribute of God's nature embodied in Jesus, which is hidden from so many.

ANGELO AND ANGELA

I'm thinking of two people right now. Angelo was a wino who lived on the streets. He was saved while still living among his homeless friends. One fateful day, he froze to death trying to keep another wino alive who had passed out in the cold.

Angelo was looked down upon by ministers who labeled him a "kook" and a religious nut. And yet, his reward in heaven is so great.

You see, in a sense, Angelo was a martyr. He was despised by many but lived every day for God. Men judged him harshly because they did not see as the Lord sees.

Angelo was born deaf. He was also abused and kept in a dark, cold attic until he was found by the authorities when he was eight years old. He had been shifted from one institution to another, where the abuse continued. Finally, he was turned out on the streets. Later in life, he gave his heart to the Lord.

The Lord gave him minimal talents, but he was faithful with what was given to him. He almost starved but refused to steal. Even though he lived in such poverty, he started spending more than half of everything he made on gospel tracts to give out on street corners because he couldn't speak.

The Lord used Angelo to lead a dying alcoholic to Him. It encouraged him so much that he would have stood on the street corner for many more years to bring another soul to repentance, but all of heaven was entreating the Lord to bring him home to receive his reward.

In heaven, he is a great king, but he could've given so much more to God's people. The churches, however, did not receive him, and ministers avoided him.

(*This story is found in Rick Joyner's book,* The Final Quest. *It is a testimony that has touched my heart many times over and continues to minister to me.*)

Now Angela is a former student of mine who is also a street preacher. She lived in her car for some time to travel all over America and preach on the streets, college campuses, and on the highways and byways of life. Now she travels to many other nations on a shoestring budget, proclaiming the gospel.

She is also one who is harshly judged because of her rough exterior and demeanor. She preaches hard and is very confrontational, but she is laying down her life for the gospel. Her level of consecration with the light she's been given puts many Christians who are living for themselves to shame.

Of course, there are many street preachers who preach the gospel with impure motives and for wrong and even perverted reasons. Equally so, there are others who are sincere, though they be unlearned and untrained. Additionally, there are many polished professional preachers who have built large churches and ministries in the name of the Lord. Some do it with pure motives, while others do it for fame and popularity. We must not judge by appearances. My point is that our glorious God does not see as we see or judge as we judge. Only He knows the true heart of a person and what light, talents, and grace He's given them to work with.

There are many who have disdain for Angela and who criticize her. But I see the work of God in her and how she pleases the Lord even with all her imperfections. I see how much she's had to overcome just to preach the gospel and travel like she does. Knowing some of her background, I see all she has forsaken to obey God. Her sacrifice and suffering have opened up a level of fellowship with the Lord in her life that few of us are familiar with. She has truly made Jesus her all in all.

It takes this kind of surrender and submission to Jesus, and suffering for the sake of the gospel, to continually experience an intimate knowledge and a holy communion with the Lord that fuels the assurance that His compassions fail not.

CHAPTER 9

THE SUFFERING SERVANT:

THE MEEKNESS OF CHRIST, THE LAMB OF GOD

I know the theme of suffering is not popular in Western Christianity, but it is a part of our calling as disciples of Jesus. Many, in their ignorance, will even rebuke any and all forms of suffering, but the Bible says differently. One preacher went so far as to foolishly proclaim that the Church today is now far more advanced than the early Church was in its embryonic state and that we don't have to suffer like they did. How some preachers manage to remain in their pulpits while spewing out such ignorant and misleading statements, I'll never know. Oh, yes — I do know: naïve and gullible people continue to grant them the authority to stay.

Jesus was our example, and He suffered many things for the sake of doing His Father's will and bringing many sons to glory (Heb. 2:10, 5:8, 9). In a similar way, we are called to jointly participate in the same hatred, ridicule, rejection, and persecution He suffered, so that we might also bring many to Him. We are called to suffer with Him (Rom. 8:17).

"For to this you were called, because Christ also suffered for us, leaving us an example, that you should follow His steps..." (1 Pt. 2:21).

We will be hated and persecuted as He was if we live as He taught us to live.

"If the world hates you, you know that it hated Me before it hated you. If you were of the world, the world would love its own. Yet because you are not of the world, but I chose you out of the world, therefore the world hates you. Remember the word that I said to you, 'A servant is not greater than his master.' If they persecuted Me, they

will also persecute you. If they kept My word, they will keep yours also. But all these things they will do to you for My name's sake, because they do not know Him who sent Me" (Jn. 15:18-21).

Jesus bore in His own body our sins, sicknesses, and diseases so that we need not suffer that way, but we are called to suffer in other ways aforementioned. But I'm afraid much of the Western Church is unprepared to suffer. We need to behold our Suffering Servant Jesus and learn to appreciate a suffering theology that will equip and prepare us to face hardship that I believe will intensify in this last hour before Jesus returns — all for the sake of others and the gospel.

Our precious Jesus was not only Deity, but He was humanity. He suffered hunger, thirst, weariness, trials, temptations, etc. — all without failing or falling. He laid aside His Deity to become a man. We often forget that.

"Let this mind be in you which was also in Christ Jesus, who, being in the form of God, did not consider it robbery to be equal with God, but made Himself of no reputation, taking the form of a bondservant, and coming in the likeness of men. And being found in appearance as a man, He humbled Himself and became obedient to the point of death, even the death of the cross" (Phil. 2:5-8).

It is the most marvelous wonder — that the Darling of Heaven humbled Himself and became a man. The pure, sinless, spotless Lamb of God came into our sin-sick, strife-filled world and served us all. He is most worthy of the reward of His sacrifice!

We are often mistaken into thinking that, because Jesus was God, He did not really suffer as we do. He is God, and we are not. To many, Jesus is just a happy remedy to their lostness and sinfulness. We dismiss the immediate relevancy of His life and words because after all, He was God. We go to heaven when we die, but His words and His acts do not bear the full impact on our souls as they ought to. Honestly, many professing Christians don't believe that Jesus was fully human — God Incarnate who lived among us. In this wistful and sentimental attitude, we develop a mindset that is unwilling to suffer, and we fall short of the scriptural admonition to *"Let this mind be in you which was also in Christ Jesus..."*

Without developing meekness in our character, we will never be willing to suffer.

THE MEEKNESS OF CHRIST

One of the meanings of "meekness" is the ability not to react in the flesh to a situation, to keep your emotions under the influence of the Holy Spirit. This ability marked the life and ministry of Jesus.

"Who is blind but My servant, or deaf as My messenger whom I send? Who is blind as he who is perfect, and blind as the Lord's servant? Seeing many things, but you do not observe; opening the ears, but he does not hear" (Is. 42:19-20).

Because of the keen spiritual sensitivity that Jesus possessed, He knew what was in the hearts of men, and, at times, by revelation, He knew what they were thinking (Mt. 9:4, 12:25) (Mk. 2:8). Yet He refused to *react* according to that knowledge of what He heard and saw and the surrounding circumstances. He maintained His position in the heavenlies, and was constantly motivated according to what the Father was saying and doing, and not man. That is meekness.

Jesus referred to Himself as meek in nature while inviting us to learn of Him.

"Come to Me, all you who labor and are heavy laden, and I will give you rest. Take My yoke upon you, and learn of Me; for I am meek and lowly in heart..." (Mt. 11:29).

How blessed and venerable is this invitation! There is no shame or intimidation in coming to the Lord. You don't have to measure up to a certain standard. To the religions of the world, Jesus speaks and says: "Come unto Me, all you who are bound by religious rituals and ceremonies that provide no peace. Come unto Me, all you who are bound by pretense and projection — trying to be someone you're not, and appeasing those who hate you, while appealing to the approval of those who can help you, and trying to impress those whom you admire. Come unto Me, all you who are tired and worn out, struggling hard and carrying heavy loads."

And what will Jesus do when you come unto Him?

He says, "I will cause you to recover your real life. I'll teach you how to take a real rest and live in that rest. I'll show you how to put off all self-sufficiency and put all your trust in Me. I'll help you recover from the heat of your burdens and teach you how to walk with Me and work with Me in the unforced rhythms of grace. You will learn to disentangle yourself from the heavy burdens of this life and everything that is not fitted for you, and you will learn to keep company with Me and live freely and lightly." (The last two paragraphs are taken from Mt. 11:29 in different Bible translations.)

What an invitation! This is the position Jesus took when He walked the earth. This was His relationship with the heavenly Father. This is the reason He could suffer according to the will of His Father.

This invitation is attractive and irresistible because of the One who is inviting you. The reason we can come to Jesus and partake of all He promises is because He is meek and lowly of heart. Unlike earthly kings and magistrates, you don't need to pay homage; you don't need to make an appointment; you don't need any special protocol. Just come as you are, and learn of Him, the meek One and lowly in heart.

By the way, "lowly in heart" literally means, "low to the ground." Metaphorically, this word signifies low estate, and lowly in position and power. Not exactly a description fit for a king. Yet Jesus was and is the greatest King.

Moses and Paul, the two most towering figures in scripture, besides Jesus, are also identified by a spirit of meekness.

"Now the man Moses was very meek, more than all men who were on the face of the earth" (Nu. 12:3).

"Now I, Paul, myself am pleading with you by the meekness and

gentleness of Christ..." (2 Cor. 10:1).

Isn't it interesting that three of the greatest men in the Bible, including Jesus, who is above all, possessed a spirit of meekness? Could this also be the reason they had such an ear for the word of the Lord, and worked so many miracles? If you don't have an ear, you don't have a mouth. Meekness and miracles are God's best combination.

"The Lord God has given me the tongue of the learned, that I should know how to speak a word in season to him who is weary: He awakens me morning by morning, He awakens mine ear to hear as the learned" (Is. 50:4).

Do you desire to walk in the blessing of an open ear? The key is in cultivating the meekness of the Lamb.

Jesus is referred to as "the Lamb" most frequently in the book of Revelation — 29 times to be exact — more than any other place in the entire Bible. There's a reason for that.

Jesus had that temper of spirit which helped Him accept the Father's dealings with Him as good and perfect and right. The Son of man did not fight against the Father. He did not struggle or contend with Him. He obeyed what the Father led Him to do without disputing or resisting. That is meekness, and thus the reason Jesus was exalted. The Lamb became the Lion.

The common assumption concerning meekness is that, when a man is meek, he cannot help himself, but the Lord was meek because He had the infinite resources of the Father at His command and still did not use them to save Himself. Why are we always trying to save ourselves, defend ourselves, and place ourselves in the best possible light in our dealings with others? Jesus had heaven's power at His disposal but He deliberately chose not to use it.

"Or do you think that I cannot now pray to My Father, and He will provide Me with more than twelve legions of angels" (Mt. 26:53)?

Oh, blessed Jesus! Who was stronger than He? He could've

destroyed His enemies with one single word. He could've called legions of angels to defend Himself and deliver Him from His oppressors, but instead He surrendered Himself to the Father's will and refused to assert His rights.

"He was oppressed and He was afflicted, yet He opened not His mouth; He was led as a lamb to the slaughter, and as a sheep before its shearers is silent, so He opened not His mouth" (Is. 53:7).

The meekness the Lamb of God possessed did not employ its authority in any coercive way. That is why He is so touchable, so approachable, and so beautiful. He will never treat you unfairly or unjustly.

Meekness is the opposite of self-assertiveness, self-interest, and self-preservation. One dictionary defines "meekness" as the equanimity of spirit that is neither elated nor cast down, simply because it is not occupied with self at all.

To many, though, meekness is too often associated with weakness. To the dominionist theologians, who aggressively assert themselves and believe that the violent take the kingdom by force, meekness is a sign of failure. They falsely believe that meekness is limp-wristedness and passivity.

Was Jesus showing Himself meek when He angrily upended the tables of the moneychangers and the seats of sellers, driving them all out of the temple (Mt. 21:12-14)? Yes, because meekness is complete obedience to God, and all the more in an act or a word that appears otherwise. One definition tells us that "meekness" does not consist in a person's outward behavior only or in his relations to his fellow man; nor is it a mere natural disposition. Rather, it is an inwrought work of the soul, whose exercises are first and chiefly toward God.

Meekness is the condition where the soul is brought into subjection and dethroned from its place as lord, so that God's voice can be heard and obeyed. Once there is a sufficient level of character development so that the spirit of a man can thus dictate to his soul, then the mind of Christ begins to be transferred to the soul of meekness. This is a miracle of great proportions, and a glowing attribute of true wisdom (Jam. 3:13).

I believe meekness to be the secret of all of God's power. It is the purest and most essential element of the character of God, and a characteristic sign of an authentic and mature apostle such as Paul. Jesus, however, is the pattern Son and our perfect example of one who possessed meekness. It was the fragrance of His life that culminated in obedience, sacrifice, and suffering, even unto the death of the cross. So few Christians possess it because they are not willing to learn of Jesus and identify with His Lamb-like qualities and sufferings.

"The Lord God has opened My ear; and I was not rebellious, nor did I turn away. I gave My back to those who struck Me, and My cheeks to those who plucked out the beard; I did not hide My face from shame and spitting" (Is. 50:4-5).

The blessing of an open ear is developed through the meekness that submitted Himself to even this kind of mockery and maltreatment.

"For to this you were called, because Christ also suffered for us, leaving us an example, that you should follow His steps: 'Who committed no sin, nor was deceit found in His mouth'; who, when He was reviled, did not revile in return; when He suffered, He did not threaten, but committed Himself to Him who judges righteously..." (1 Pt. 2:21-23).

The key to Jesus' submission and restraint lay in the knowledge He possessed that the real power and authority did not lie in the hands of His enemies, of men or kings, or the Roman soldiers who crucified Him, but in the hands of the Almighty Father. We catch a glimpse of this when Jesus said to Pilate: *"You could have no power at all against Me unless it had been given you from above"* (Jn. 19:11). At one point, Pilate marveled at Jesus' silence and refusal to defend Himself in the face of so many lies and false accusations (Mt. 27:14). Jesus had already submitted His will to the Father and knew that Pilate was simply a human instrument in the Father's hand to accomplish His perfect will.

Meekness can be developed sooner in our lives when we finally realize that God is working out His sovereign will on our behalf, and every person and situation we encounter in life is simply a tool to help accomplish that, even when it seems unjust. We must see the hand behind the tool and surrender to Him and His dealings in our lives.

Moses and Paul, whom I referred to earlier as some great Biblical examples of meekness, did not start out meek, and neither do we. Quite the opposite. They both learned hard lessons — Moses on the back side of the desert when he asserted himself to kill an Egyptian who was oppressing a Hebrew and then had to flee for his life when it was discovered (Ex. 2); and Paul (Saul), who was a fighter and a defender of the Jewish religion. He fought for the right of the Jewish people and even traveled long distances to arrest Christians, imprison them, and have them killed. But God dealt with both Moses and Paul (Saul), who, having learned many painful lessons, were gradually transformed through them. They learned not to do things in their own strength and according to their own will. Both became very meek as the Scriptures testify. Paul learned to be content in all circumstances, whether good or bad. He learned the meekness of Christ.

While Moses serves as a great Old Testament example of meekness, Jonah was quite the opposite. God had to fight Jonah for every inch of submission and obedience. He was very stubborn and assertive and fought for his own way and tried to make God conform to his selfish will and desires. As a result, Jonah never learned meekness and never really found peace and contentment. Yet he was a genuine prophet of God. We have many ministers today who have never learned meekness. What a contrast between Moses and Jonah! What a contrast between Paul and Jonah! Are you a Paul or a Jonah?

The turning point in Paul's life came when the Lord appeared to him and first spoke to him, saying: *"It is hard for you to kick against the goads"* (Acts 9:5). Herein is a great word for all believers, especially many American believers, who are used to being pampered and coaxed into believing that all suffering must be resisted.

Goads were attached to the front of carts to teach oxen not to kick against the cart but to bring them to a point of submission to do the will of their master. It was only the oxen who had not learned submission and meekness that kicked against the goads. Similarly, Christians who are constantly frustrated and agitated because things don't go their way have not learned true meekness and are fighting against the very things the Lord is using to guide them and train them.

In countries where oxen are still used to pull carts or plows, the younger, wilder oxen are often teamed up and yoked with the older, more mature oxen, for the purpose that the younger will be tamed by the older. In the same way, Jesus invites us to take His yoke upon us that we may learn meekness from Him. There is some suffering in the flesh that we will experience on the way to cultivating meekness in our lives. If we fight against it, we will not grow in meekness, but, instead, we will continue to experience frustration and aggravation as our painful experiences lose their value and become counterproductive. Thus, we will remain in the wilderness, so to speak, and have to keep learning and relearning the same lessons, thereby stunting our spiritual growth.

I'm afraid many of us have not been conditioned to suffer. Quite the contrary. The American Church has been conditioned to avoid suffering at all costs. Yet many of the great souls that have been called and planted by the Lord have experienced suffering, especially in antichrist nations, where there is great persecution. It was the pain of suffering that conferred great character and strength on their faith.

Not only are we conditioned not to suffer, but there seems to be little place given to chastisement, brokenness, a contrite heart, poverty of soul, and godly sorrow in the Church and in our society today. Instead, our culture breeds pride, arrogance, and a sense of entitlement. We love control, and we tend to glory in our fleshly achievements and successes; this attitude has infiltrated much of the Church.

It seems that in today's "let's get motivated to succeed" crazed culture within the Church, too few have taken the time to discover the truth, the purpose, and the significant role that suffering plays when it comes to our solid spiritual growth and development in Christ.

I've been around persecuted Christians and have received much from their spirit. When you are around someone who suffers, there is an aroma of Christ that pervades the very atmosphere. Listen to the words of Watchmen Nee describe the breaking of the alabaster box by the woman who anointed Jesus for burial (Jn. 12:1-8):

"The breaking of the alabaster box and the anointing of the Lord filled the house with the sweetest odor. Everyone could smell it. Whenever you meet someone who has really suffered — been limited, gone through things for the Lord, been imprisoned, and is satisfied with the Lord and nothing else — immediately you sense the fragrance. There is a savor of the Lord. Something has been crushed. Something has been broken. And there is a resulting odor of sweetness."

Jesus was broken. Jesus was crushed. He suffered as a man and not as God. For this reason, He is called "the Lamb of God."

BEHOLD THE LAMB!

Jesus is called "the Lamb of God" — a title and description of Him that is so otherworldly. The Son of God — who co-existed eternally with the Father in glory, the One who was from the beginning, without whom nothing was made, for *"all things were made through Him, and without Him nothing was made that was made"* (Jn. 1:3) — this God became a Lamb, a baby sheep, the weakest and meekest of all animals, whose meat is known for its delicate flavor and tender flesh.

"Knowing that you were not redeemed with corruptible things, like silver and gold...but with the precious blood of Christ, as of a lamb without blemish and without spot" (1 Pt. 1:18-19).

In the gospel of John, it was John the Baptist who first saw Jesus as the Lamb of God (Jn. 1:29, 36). As already stated, the book of

Revelation is unique in its repetitive reference to "the Lamb." In a vision, John the beloved saw a Lamb, signifying the Christ of God. The book of Revelation also portrays four living creatures and twenty-four elders who fall before the Lamb, singing praise for His purchase of all people with His own blood (Rev. 5:9).

On the night God's people were to depart out of Egypt, where they were slaves, and go into the Promised Land, the firstborn in all the Egyptian families died. The firstborn of the Israelites, however, were saved because God had instructed them to kill a lamb and mark their doorposts with its blood (Ex. 12). The angel of death then knew to pass over those houses.

The Israelites ate the "Passover" lamb in one meal (one sitting) before they departed. The lamb was to have no blemish and none of its bones were to be broken. To this day, the Jews remember this night as the Feast of Passover. After Jesus' crucifixion, soldiers did not break his legs to kill Him because he was already dead. Like the Passover lamb, His bones were not broken.

At Calvary, the Lamb of God submitted to the will of the Father to be slain but now is trusted with the judgment of mankind and given a Name above all names. The Messianic prophecy reads, *"Though he was harshly treated, he submitted and opened not his mouth; like a lamb led to the slaughter"* (Is. 53:7).

Behold the Lamb when He stood before Herod and uttered not a word in defense. *"Then he questioned Him with many words, but He answered nothing"* (Lk. 23:9). Then, again, He was questioned before Pilate, and still He kept silent. *"But Jesus gave him no answer"* (Lk. 19:9). He knew He was the Lamb, and He knew He was born to die to redeem mankind.

The Lamb's death on the cross defeated spiritual death in all of us. His crucifixion caused death to pass over us and for life to be granted. By His blood we are saved from death. Jesus, the Lamb of God, made it possible for us to be free from the slavery of sin and death. Isn't it interesting and even surreal that the day of Jesus' crucifixion was the same day the Passover lambs were also being killed in the Temple on Preparation Day (Jn. 19:31)?

Behold the Lamb in Gethsemane! Behold Him in the garden of His greatest trial as He sweat great drops of blood! Behold Him at the scourging post! Behold His desire to drink the cup when His flesh and natural man cried out against it! With the horrors of His separation from the Father facing Him, behold how He prayed that the Father's will would be done!

We are commanded to eat the Lamb's flesh and blood (Jn. 6:53) to receive eternal life and are to continue to feed on that life all our days, just as Jesus fed on the life of the Father through His obedience. The meat of obedience was the Lamb's food. The meat of obedience was the core value of His entire life. Even when He was seen in the temple at 12 years of age, he was surprised to find that His parents did not know that He was about His Father's business.

The great delight of the Lamb was to do the Father's will. He had no desire to initiate any action or assignment outside of the will of His Father. The Lamb's love for the Father manifested even to the obedience of the death of the cross. Obedience is the manifestation of not only love for the Father (Jn. 15) but of the fear of the Lord. These next three verses, one in two different translations, bear witness to another outstanding quality of the life of the Lamb — the fear of the Lord, which always culminates in obedience.

"His delight is in the fear of the Lord" (Is. 11:3).

"His greatest joy will be to obey the Lord" (Is. 11:3 — CEV). Notice how "the fear of the Lord" is translated into "obedience."

...The Father has not left Me alone; for I do always those things that please Him" (Jn. 8:29).

"Sacrifice and offering You did not desire; My ears You have opened. Burnt offering and sin offering You did not require. Then I said, 'Behold, I come; In the scroll of the book it is written of me. I delight to do Your will, O my God, and Your law is within my heart'"

(Ps. 40:6-8).

The love of obedience marked the Lamb's life and will mark the mature sons of God.

How beautiful are these qualities of Jesus, the Lamb of God!

CHAPTER 10

JESUS: THE EXPRESS IMAGE OF THE LOVE OF THE FATHER

Jesus says that anyone who has seen Him has seen the Father (Jn. 14:9), for He is the outshining or *the brightness of the Father's glory and the express image of His Person"* (Heb. 1:3), and *"the image of the invisible God"* (Col. 1:15). If Jesus was not the Son of God and had not existed in eternity past in the Father's bosom, He could not reveal His glory unto us.

"And now, Father, glorify Me together with Yourself, with the glory which I had with You before the world was" (Jn. 17:5).

Because He was intimate with the Father and freely shared the Father's glory with us, we can also know Him with that same kind of intimacy that no other god could ever give.

The emphasis of the Christian life is not primarily about lifestyle change. Lifestyle change is a byproduct of knowing God, which is eternal life (Jn. 17:3). To know God intimately and to enjoy Him is what we were created for. So many miss that.

A hunger and desire for God is what alters our behavior and changes our preferences and the choices we make in life. But in order to desire God, we must *find* Him desirable. To many, He is not, because they have not seen Him as He is. To many, He is distant, boring, and a killjoy. This is the reason I have also included a chapter on His majesty and condescension, and the compassions of His great heart. This book, however, wouldn't be complete without putting a greater emphasis on the fact that God is a very deeply loving God and Father (1 Jn. 4:8-9). This, above all else, is what makes Him irresistibly desirable and infinitely beautiful. My prayer is that you may learn to behold the beauty of His glory. This is the Father that Jesus was one with and came to declare to us. David, a type of Christ in the Old

Testament, spoke this by revelation.

"One thing I have desired of the Lord, that will I seek: that I may dwell in the house of the Lord all the days of my life, to behold the beauty of the Lord, and to inquire in His temple" (Ps. 27:4).

God is not only eternal but personable, interesting, and fascinating. Once we see Him as He is, we will leave all the preconceived notions we've ever had of Him behind. We will trade our intellectual, abstract view of a "general" God for the loving and beautiful and personable Father that He is. He is the God and Father of His beloved Son Jesus, and He is our God and Father, too, and calls us "beloved."

Jesus said to her, "Do not cling to Me, for I have not yet ascended to My Father; but go to My brethren and say to them, 'I am ascending to My Father and your Father, and to My God and your God'" (Jn. 20:17).

Before God is the Creator or the Almighty Ruler, He is Father. It's when we see that, even in creating and ruling, He does so as a kind and loving Father, we are moved to such joy and delight at the thought of being His children. The God who is love (1 Jn. 4:8) is a Father who sent His Son, so we could all, in turn, be sons. To be the Father means to love, it means to give life, it means to beget the Son, and to share His Son and now His Spirit with us all. In eternity past, before anything else was, God was loving, giving life, and delighting in His Son. This is what filled the heart of Jesus and is the reason He could say the following:

"The Father loves the Son, and has given all things into His hand" (Jn. 3:35).

"For the Father loves the Son, and shows Him all things that He Himself does..." (Jn. 5:20).

The Father's love is always primary, but the Son reciprocates with love that manifests in obedience.

"But that the world may know that I love the Father, and as the Father gave Me commandment, so I do" (Jn. 14:31).

As already stated, the Son loves the Father so much that it is His sheer joy and delight to do the Father's will and pleasure. He called it His "food."

Jesus said to them, *"My food is to do the will of Him who sent Me, and to finish His work"* (Jn. 4:34).

"I delight to do Your will, O my God, and Your law is within my heart" (Ps. 40:8).

Jesus was nourished from doing the Father's will. It was delightful for Him to obey the Father. The Father's love motivated Him. Along with the fear of the Lord, this love is also to be the motivating factor in our lives to do the Father's will.

This is the same love that Jesus shared with His disciples and what He expects us to share with others.

"A new commandment I give to you, that you love one another; as I have loved you, that you also love one another" (Jn. 13:34).

"As the Father loved Me, I also have loved you..." (Jn. 15:9).

The Father's eternal love for the Son excites the Son's responsive eternal love for the Father, and His eternal love flows freely to His disciples and now to His Church. By this, one may see how the Christian life is to be lived. Without this exchange and free flow of love, there is no joy and delight in the heart and in our service.

"We love Him because He first loved us" (1 Jn. 4:19). Love is the fuel and the oxygen of life in God. If you're not receiving His love, you cannot release His love. It's that simple.

Many know God only as a Creator and a Judge. Others have a crooked perspective of Him and see Him as a sort of policeman or traffic cop who springs into action only when they are caught in a wrongdoing. It's like an acquaintance of mine who introduced me one day to his friends, saying, "This is Bert Farias, a man who would like to do as he pleases and live like us, but he cannot because he is a minister." How demeaning a view of God and His amazing grace that some people have! This acquaintance of mine at the time was a recovering alcoholic who was attending AA, hoping to overcome his addiction. Without an intimate knowledge of the Father's love, we will be left to serve Him in our own strength and will-power, which will always fail.

Without the Lord Jesus coming into our world as God Incarnate, living among us, and revealing the deepest profundity of the fatherly heart of God, this is the conclusion many mere humans will formulate of Him. This perception of God does not draw me close. It does not pull on my heartstrings. It does not stir up any desire to know Him. This demeaning view of God is not enough. Unless we come to know Him as a loving Father, we will have a crippling walk with God and be at a grave disadvantage in relation to Him. We will never function aright until we see Him aright.

This is the God Jesus reflected. This is the Father He came to reveal to us.

Just the singular fact that, through sending His Son, the Father has reconciled us unto Himself, reveals the inexpressibly loving and supreme tenderness of His fatherly nature. Reading and reflecting on the beautiful account of the prodigal son should cure our orphan hearts once and for all (Lk. 15:11-32). In the story, the father waited for his wayward and rebellious son to come home. When he finally did, notice what kind of reception he received — far from that which an irate policeman, an angry traffic cop, or a vindictive judge would give.

"And he arose and came to his father. **But when he was still a great way off, his father saw him and had compassion, and ran and fell on his neck and kissed him.** *And the son said to him, 'Father, I have sinned against heaven and in your sight, and am no longer worthy to be called your son.'*

"But the father said to his servants, 'Bring out the best robe and

put it on him, and put a ring on his hand and sandals on his feet. And bring the fatted calf here and kill it, and let us eat and be merry; for this my son was dead and is alive again; he was lost and is found.' And they began to be merry" (Lk. 15:20-24).

I imagine that this prodigal's father was out there every day expecting his son's return for *"when he was still a great way off, his father saw him."* He knew his son's walk, his frame, and the shape of his body, and recognized him from afar. Now observing his youngest son bowed over with defeat and the ravages of sin, the father ran out to meet him and fell on his neck and kissed him even before he could confess his sin. This is one of the clearest and most affectionate pictures of the heart of our heavenly Father, whom Jesus came to portray. In this great salvation is a God we can truly and easily love. He is Father to those who've received His Son.

This tender depiction of our Father is what brings us great joy and assurance and wins and warms our hearts to His. How boundlessly He loves us! Taste of His merciful, generous, and benevolent heart that the Son has revealed unto us.

"All things have been delivered to Me by My Father, and no one knows the Son except the Father. Nor does anyone know the Father except the Son, and the one to whom the Son wills to reveal Him" (Mt. 11:27).

Once the prodigal son came to his senses, returned home, and confessed his sin, I'm sure that his father never reminded him of his sin and transgression again. That is the devil's nature, for he is called *"the accuser of the brethren"* (Rev. 12:10); it is not the nature of a true father. Once we confess our sins, He will not remember them.

"I, even I, am He who blots out your transgressions for My own sake; and I will not remember your sins" (Is. 43:25).

But did you ever notice that this God blots out our transgressions *for His own sake?* That seems to make no sense. I thought He blotted out our transgressions for our sake. After all, we were the ones who were in bondage to sin. How could God have blotted out our transgressions for *His* own sake?

It's because our sins separated us from God (Is. 59:2), and He could not fellowship with us. He could not come to us. The chasm of sin separated us from Him. No father enjoys being separated from His children but longs for their fellowship. How much more does the heavenly Father long for us! This is what Jesus came to show us — that He and the Father were one in their quest for man. Oh, beloved, He wants us! He chose us. And Jesus became the bridge back to our Father — the way, the truth, and the life.

Think on the grandness and greatness of God for a moment with respect to the universe. There is a passage in Isaiah 40 that paints this picture. Let's highlight a few verses that show us the unlimited magnitude of His omnipotence in creation and His infinite knowledge.

"Who has measured the water in the hollow of His hand, measured heaven with a span and calculated the dust of the earth in a measure? Weighed the mountains in scales and the hills in a balance? (v. 12)

"Behold, the nations are as a drop in a bucket, and are counted as the small dust on the scales; look, He lifts up the isles as a very little thing. (v. 15)

"All nations before Him are as nothing, and they are counted by Him less than nothing and worthless." (v. 17)

Are you getting the picture?

Now think of planet Earth in relation to the universe and millions of galaxies out there that God spoke into existence and that are still expanding. What is the Earth in the midst of such but a tiny dot? Now think of the United States or the nation you live in compared to the rest of the Earth. If the Earth is a small dot in comparison to the universe, then the USA or your nation is a very small portion of that dot. Now think of the state or region you actually live in, in reference to both the Earth and the USA or nation of your residence. It's getting smaller in proportion, isn't it?

Now think of your town or city. It's just a tiny speck in comparison to all we've described. Go even further. Think of the street and the house you live in. We are looking now at the speck of a speck of a speck.

Now see yourself in one room of your house in proportion to the entire universe and creation of God I've highlighted here. Now you are a very tiny speck of a tiny speck of a tiny speck. Yet this great and omnipotent God, who is unlimited in His power and knowledge, has chosen to send Jesus Christ to the Earth to shed His blood in order to blot out our sins and transgressions, so that His Spirit could dwell in you and me — so that He could actually make His home in our hearts. Wow! That is boundless, amazing love, which fuels us with unspeakable joy and deep assurance. That is as close as I can get to describing His longing to fellowship with you — that your body would actually be His temple and the house He lives in (1 Cor. 6:19). Praise God and glory to His Name forevermore!

When I was meditating on these thoughts one day, starting from Isaiah 40, this song rose up in my heart by the Spirit of God.

Thou art great, oh God

Thou art so great, my God

Thou art far above the heavens

And high above all gods

Thou hast measured the waters in the hollow of thine hand,

And meted out heaven with a span

Thou hast comprehended the dust of the earth in a measure,

And weighed the mountains in scales and the hills in a balance.

Behold, the nations are as a drop of a bucket in thy sight,

And are counted as the small dust of the balance,

And You take up the islands as a very little thing.

Thou art so high and great, oh God

Yet You walk with me

You speak to me and commune with me.

Oh, wonder of wonders and glory of glories

That You would drink sin's bitter cup

So that I could wear a crown

You lifted me so high up

By coming so far down

All so You could commune with me again.

The moment I did discover

That You were this kind of lover

I gave You my heart

Now I don't want to sleep

Because my longing is so deep

Just to know You, Lord.

Lord Jesus, I love you...

The Father and the Son, along with the Holy Spirit, worked together to accomplish this great plan of redemption. How blessed we are to be loved and valued by Him and to be called the children of God.

"Behold what manner of love the Father has bestowed on us, that we should be called children of God!" (1 Jn. 3:1).

Love never fails. Love always wins.

This is our God. This is our Father. This is His Son who has revealed Him unto us.

This is the real Jesus.

CHAPTER 11

THE HOLY SPIRIT MAKES JESUS REAL

Jesus shed His holy blood to redeem us from our sinful state. His resurrection was His signature and final, infallible proof of His reality, but His ascension and His seating at the right hand of the Father sealed the covenant that we might receive the fullness of His Spirit.

The beginning of this fullness originated in Acts 2:4, when those 120 waiting disciples were immersed in the power of the Spirit and spoke in other tongues as they were given utterance.

Notice that the apostles attributed the entire event to Jesus from His exalted seat of power.

"This Jesus God has raised up, of which we are all witnesses. Therefore being exalted to the right hand of God, and having received from the Father the promise of the Holy Spirit, He poured out this which you now see and hear" (Acts 2:32-33).

The promise of the mighty baptism in the Holy Spirit gives us a deeper revelation of the exalted Lordship of Jesus Christ.

Here are some other chief functions of the Holy Spirit Jesus foretold: *"He will teach you all things, and bring to your remembrance all things that I said to you"* (Jn. 14:26); *"He will guide you into all truth...he will show you things to come"* (Jn. 16:13); *"He will take of what is Mine and declare it unto you"* (Jn. 16:14-15); *"He will testify of Me"* (Jn. 15:26), and *"He will glorify Me"* (Jn. 16:14). When I was a young Christian, these verses did not register on my spirit like they do now, after decades of walking with the Lord. The Holy Spirit has enlarged my heart through revelation. He has made Jesus bigger to me. This is what the baptism of the Holy Spirit — with the frequent use of praying in other tongues — does.

What a difference from the Old Covenant era, when men needed a prophet, a spokesman, a leader, or rabbi to guide them. In His Earth walk, Jesus was all those things to His disciples and more. Now, under the New Covenant dispensation, men can have a spirit-to-Spirit relationship and fellowship with God. After multiple post-resurrection appearances to present Himself alive *"by many infallible proofs"* (Act 1:3), the relationship between Jesus and His disciples changed and would no longer depend on His geographical proximity to them. The Holy Spirit, also referred to as the Helper, would now take the place of Jesus on the Earth and reveal His glory to us.

"And I will pray the Father, and He will give you another Helper..." (Jn. 14:16). The word *"another"* means: "One besides; another of the same kind." The word shows similarities but also diversities of operations and ministries. The Word Wealth in my New Spirit Filled Life Bible says it like this: Jesus' use of this word for sending another Comforter equals "one besides Me and in addition to Me but One just like Me. He will do in My absence what I would do if I were physically present with you." The Spirit's coming assures continuity with what Jesus did and taught.

Where once the disciples were baffled by Jesus' parables and sayings (*"We do not know what He is saying.* [Jn. 16:18] *Lord, we do not know where You are going. How can we know the way?"* [Jn. 14:5] etc.), now, after Pentecost, they were empowered and emboldened, for they knew the One who had departed from them had returned in the form of Another like Him, whom He also called the Comforter. The identity of Jesus the Christ became clear to them, as well as His plan, purpose, and great commission. But they were not only empowered and emboldened by the Spirit, but now as citizens of another homeland called heaven, they received their heavenly language. They were now part of another kingdom that required another language, "kingdom linguistics" if you will — a brand-new, not *mother tongue*, but *Father tongue*. *"For he who speaks in a tongue does not speak to men but to God* (the Father)" (1 Cor. 14:2). I liken the new birth to a passport to heaven, for one must be born again to enter (Jn. 3:5), but the baptism in the Holy Spirit with the evidence of speaking in other tongues is our *kingdom language* here on the Earth.

Many believers are content with the passport but don't seem to care too much about the new language by which they can communicate with God on a higher spiritual dimension, one that bypasses their intellect. Today, many believers have been hoodwinked by the devil and injected with unbelief concerning the mighty baptism in the Spirit. The tongues have been the primary subject of controversy for centuries, and yet it is our key to revelation knowledge. How do you suppose the apostle Paul received revelation to pen more than half of the New Testament? It was because of this statement.

"I thank my God I speak with tongues more than you all" (1 Cor. 14:18).

That was his secret to revelation knowledge. That was his secret to the intimate knowledge he received of Jesus from the Holy Spirit. Having never walked in physical form with Him as the other original apostles had, yet I believe he possessed a deeper knowledge of the *"unsearchable riches of Christ"* than perhaps any of them did. But no one can challenge the fact of the post-Pentecost spiritual advancement and progress of the original apostles, too. Those uneducated and untrained Galilean men confounded the religious leaders of their day, for they realized that they had been with Jesus (Acts 4:13). It wasn't just His resurrection and ascension that was the basis for their transformation but the outpouring of the Spirit's power from heaven, inclusive of tongues. They now possessed a heightened consciousness of Jesus and His role in time and eternity. He was real; He was alive — not only because He appeared to them but because of Pentecost. There is no other plausible explanation. The baptism in the Holy Spirit with evidential tongues, which constitutes your heavenly prayer language, is the great key to revelation knowledge and enlarging your vision of Jesus.

The contrast between these early apostles in the gospels versus the book of Acts cannot be explained any other way except to say that something powerful happened to the 120 on the day of Pentecost that totally revolutionized their lives. Their revelation of Jesus Christ had been ignited, enlarged, and expanded by their Pentecostal experience. The Holy Spirit had unveiled to them the personal and eternal reality of Jesus, and they were endued with power.

The work of the Spirit is to feature Jesus and present Him in His glory. As we are filled and refilled with the Spirit, He baptizes us continually into the implications of who Jesus is. But it all begins with the Holy Spirit falling on us in the initial baptism as *"at the beginning"* (Acts 11:15).

What is known in theology as Biblical glossolalia (tongues) is produced within the core of one's inner being. It's not just gibberish. When you submit your total being to the Lord, of which your tongue is the most unruly member, the Spirit produces utterances that are voiced in cooperation with your faith in Christ's Lordship. Such holy speech builds one up, but the mind often rebels at the mystery of it, thus necessitating a deepening dependence and childlike faith in giving action to the utterance you sense. At the same time, as you yield to the Lord and the Spirit's work, an incomparable freedom of expression will be released, which expands with yielding and use.

Here's a testimony of a college senior that testifies to this invaluable Christ-centered dimension of the Spirit's baptism:

"In my own life, praying in tongues has made me more responsive to the Lordship of Jesus. When I yield my tongue to His control, my heart experiences an intimate communion with Him. I am free to let the Spirit of God pray through me in His own way, to let Him pray for His perfect will. Those who analyze tongues without ever having yielded their speech to the Lordship of His Holy Spirit cannot begin to comprehend the depths of God; it is foolishness to them!"

May Jesus be magnified in your life and made more real through this sacred baptism in the Spirit and the extensive use of speaking and praying in other tongues.

CONCLUSION

What God is like our God, who is completely just and could deal with the Earth in wrath and anger as He needs to, and yet so merciful that He would wait and wait and wait for sinners to repent, well beyond the patience that you or I could ever have? And if that were not enough, God, in the person of Jesus Christ, came in our weakly human form to die our death for us, so that we who deserved it, don't get what we deserve, and He who did not deserve it got what we deserve.

That is a beautiful Man.

A scholar once stated that if Jesus had never lived, we would never have been able to invent Him. This is true.

Some scholars think Jesus is a copy of this myth from some people group, and that the entire gospel is a copy from this myth, or a manufactured tale of some dreamer from a distant time. But this Incarnate God is no myth or product of a mystical dream from philosophers of a different day. Jesus was not copied or created by imagination. It is impossible to find another like Him. One cannot combine the beauty of the balance of justice and mercy, and grace and truth, that lived the way He lived. No human mind or ingenuity could make Him up.

We have telescopes that have supposedly seen what is called dark matter, which means we know that the matter is there, but we don't know what it is. And scientists have supposedly found this dark energy, which means we know that this energy is there, but we don't know what it is. And these scientists and astronomers tell us that we don't really know what constitutes 96% of reality. Yet these so-called experts have the audacity to think they have enough evidence to say there is no God and that Jesus Christ is a myth.

The unlimited beauty, perfection, life, and glory in Jesus, the Man, are beyond human imagination and myth. It cannot be thought up, explained, or reasoned. Who could imagine a God who would come among His people and die their death, but before doing so, would serve them? Who would do that with no guarantee that the people He created would believe in Him or follow Him? Who would do that without insisting you recognize who He really is?

There is no man like that Man! When you find a Man like that, you have found God. When you find a Man like that, you have found a treasure hidden in a field and a pearl of great price.

"Again, the kingdom of heaven is like treasure hidden in a field, which a man found and hid; and for joy over it he goes and sells all that he has and buys that field" (Mt. 13:44).

Wonderful Jesus is the treasure hidden in the field. In Him I have found all that I'll ever need. To me, that means the following:

No more looking for the accolades of men and finding fulfillment in people. No more hiding behind a false, projected image. No more pretenses. No more twisting words, events, and situations to place myself in the best possible light. No more positioning or posturing myself to gain a personal advantage or to court man's favor. No more taking the higher seat. No more need to build something for God or be a success in the eyes of man. No more needing to feel useful. No more operating in a performance mode for the acceptance and approval of man. No more trying to keep up with my peers to prove my worth in life and ministry. No more searching for ways to please people. No more trying to think or reason my way out of hardship or difficulties.

I have found what I'm looking for. My treasure is Jesus. I am in the process of selling everything I have to buy the field for the treasure therein. I am full of joy for the treasure that I am digging out.

I have found my One Pearl of Great Price (v. 45-46); He is my Lord Jesus Christ. This one pearl is precious and priceless, and I cannot live without Him. He's not only my personal Savior and Lord but the best friend I ever had.

Oh, that all mankind would discover this Pearl of Great Price!

ABOUT THE AUTHOR

Bert M. Farias, together with his wife Carolyn, graduates of Rhema Bible Training Center, founded Holy Fire Ministries in 1997 after serving for nine years as missionaries in West Africa, establishing nation-changing interdenominational Bible training centers with an organization called Living Word Missions.

From 1999 to 2003, Bert served as the internship coordinator on the senior leadership team of the Brownsville Revival School of Ministry and Fire School of Ministry in Pensacola, Florida, a school birthed from a massive heaven-sent revival that brought approximately four million visitors from around the world, with an estimated 150,000 first-time conversions. There, Rev. Farias and his wife taught and mentored young men and women in the call of God, training them for the work of the ministry.

Bert is a messenger of the Lord, carrying a spirit of revival to the Church and the nations. An anointing of fire marks His ministry with frequent demonstrations of the Spirit and the power of God. With a divine commission to also write, Bert has authored several books with an emphasis on helping to restore the real spirit of Christianity in the Church today and preparing the saints for the glory of God, the harvest, and the imminent return of the Lord.

Before being separated to the full-time preaching and teaching ministry, Bert experienced a unique and powerful baptism of fire. His consuming passion is for human beings to come into a real and vibrant relationship with the Lord Jesus Christ through the power of the Holy Spirit and to become passionate workers in His kingdom, thus preparing them for the second coming of Christ, being among the wise virgins and a part of the first-fruits harvest who will gain an abundant entrance into glory and receive a sure reward.

Bert currently resides in Windham, New Hampshire, with his beautiful wife Carolyn. They are proud parents of one precious son of promise.

MINISTRY INFORMATION

To become a monthly partner with Holy Fire Ministries, schedule a speaking engagement with Bert and/or Carolyn, receive a free monthly newsletter, or follow Bert's blog, please visit our website: **www.holy-fire.org**

HOLY FIRE MINISTRIES

PO Box 4527

Windham, NH 03087

Email: adm@holy-fire.org

OTHER BOOKS BY BERT M. FARIAS*

SOULISH LEADERSHIP

PURITY OF HEART

THE JOURNAL OF A JOURNEY TO HIS HOLINESS

THE REAL SPIRIT OF REVIVAL

THE REAL SALVATION

THE REAL GOSPEL

MY SON, MY SON: FATHERING AND TRAINING A HOLY GENERATION

PRAYER: THE LANGUAGE OF THE SPIRIT

PASSING ON THE MOVE OF GOD TO THE NEXT GENERATION

*To order any of these books or to view a synopsis of them, visit our website or Amazon books.

*If this book or any of Bert's other books have been a blessing to you, kindly post a review on Amazon.

Made in the USA
Columbia, SC
05 February 2018